HANDLING
CARGO

HANDLING CARGO

FREIGHTERS OF THE 1950s AND '60s

WILLIAM H. MILLER

The History Press

Front cover: Brocklebank Line's *Mangla* in the River Hoogly near
Calcutta (by Stephen Card)
Back cover: The *Brisbane Star* at Southampton (Kenneth Wrightsman,
courtesy of Mike Lindsay)

First published 2018

The History Press
The Mill, Brimscombe Port
Stroud, Gloucestershire, GL5 2QG
www.thehistorypress.co.uk

British Library Cataloguing in Publication Data.
A catalogue record for this book is available from the British Library.

ISBN 978 0 7509 8434 8

Typesetting and origination by The History Press
Printed and bound in India by Thomson Press India Ltd.

Contents

Dedication

To my dear friend Dr Nico Guns,
who has done exceptional work in documenting Dutch shipping, especially passenger ships.
A great salute to him!

Foreword

I met Bill Miller on the *Queen Mary 2* and enjoyed his lectures about the great ocean liners. They brought back many memories. But in my younger days, I served on cargo ships. Compared to the glamorous liners, I think of those freighters as 'working ships'. They carried all sorts of cargos from one place to another – with erratic schedules, sometimes long stays in remote ports and sometimes sailing in the middle of the night. Rarely were there set schedules.

Myself, I sailed mostly with the Blue Star Line. Now gone from the seas, they were an excellent company with many excellent ships. I had stints on the *Argentina Star, Uruguay Star, Wellington Star* and *Brisbane Star*. Some voyages took months, but I was young then, in the sixties, and it was a great way to see the world.

I am honoured to write this foreword for Bill's book on those now bygone freighters. It was a great era with great ships. Thank you, Bill, for reminding us.

Jim Mason
Liverpool, England

Acknowledgements

Like one of these freighters, it takes many hands to create a book like this. My sincere appreciation to all. Special mention to Stephen Card for his artwork and to Mick Lindsay for generously sharing his vast photo collection and those of Kenneth Wrightman and Dave Vincent. Further thanks to Jim Mason for his foreword.

Special mention to Gordon Cooper, Anthony Las Forgia and Alan Parkhurst.

Further acknowledgement is given to Robert Capello, Michael Cassar, Priscilla Corbett, Richard Faber, Mr and Mrs Henry Dahl, Captain W.J. Deijnen, the late Alex Duncan, the late John Gillespie, Dr Nico Guns, Alan Hulse, Des Kirkpatrick, Arnold Kludas, Norman Knebel, Vincent Love, Miles MacMahon, John Malone, Captain James McNamara, Hisashi Noma, Geoff Palmer, Helen Routledge, James L. Shaw, Martin Shawcross, the late Captain Cornelius van Herk and Laurent van der Laan.

Companies and organisations that have assisted include American President Lines, Blue Funnel Line, Ellerman Lines, Grace Line, Moore-McCormack Lines, Moran Towing & Transportation Co., Port Authority of New York & New Jersey, Port of London Authority, Royal Netherlands Steamship Co., Steamship Historical Society of America, United Fruit Co., United States Lines, World Ocean & Cruise Liner Society and World Ship Society.

Any oversight is mine and deeply regretted.

Introduction

It was the end of an era, just before the massive transition to faster, more efficient containerised shipping and on larger and larger vessels. Freighters of the fifties and sixties – with masts, booms and hatches – were the last of their generation. They were 'working ships'. To me, they were also very interesting ships. And to me, they had character, charm and a sense of industry and commerce. They had a sense of romance about them – ships that carried all sorts of goods and sailed off to interesting and faraway places. And uniquely, they were also passenger ships, not liners, but many carried up to a dozen passengers, the maximum allowed under international maritime law without having an on-board doctor.

This is a scrapbook of sorts for me – a collection of as many freighters as I could include under the limitations of a single book. Many companies, such as Fred Olsen, German-Africa and the Knutsen Line, have not, quite sadly, been included. In some instances, I had histories, reflections, notations and especially personal anecdotes to share. And, of course, the photographs – taken from many sources and collections.

Sadly, many of these ships would be retired prematurely from the services of well-known shipping lines and finish up under flags of convenience, for virtually unknown owners, before going off, usually to Indian and Pakistani scrappers, in the seventies and eighties. For some ships, their life's work was cut short and their decommissioning was quite quick.

For me, this is a true voyage down maritime memory lane. There are the likes of Cunard, Holland America and United States Shipping Lines on the North Atlantic, Moore-McCormack lines to South America, Farrell lines to Africa and P&O out to the east. Closer to home, I can well remember a summer's afternoon over fifty years ago, in the 1960s. In New York Harbor there might be six or even seven American Export-Isbrandtsen freighters at Hoboken, and nearby one or two immaculate Holland America ships. And at nearby Jersey City, two big American President Lines ships. Across the Hudson and over in Manhattan, several United Fruit Company ships were readying to cast off by, say, Friday afternoon. Then ships of the Venezuelan Line, Argentine State Line and a couple of freighters from Moore-McCormack Lines. Farther north in Chelsea, there would be three Grace Line and four or five United States Lines ships. And in the Hudson itself, one of the big, Mariner-class ships belonging to American Pioneer Line might be arriving while one of the smart-looking Norwegian-flag vessels, operated by the Cosmopolitan Line, sailed off and picked up speed. Yes, an exciting era – and, visually, plentiful times.

So, the cargo has been loaded, the booms stowed and the lines released – a freighter is about to depart. The whistle is sounding. Turn the pages – pages along which maritime memory lane begins.

Bill Miller
Secaucus, New Jersey

1

Tulips from Holland and Wines from Italy: Transatlantic Routes

United States Lines

Usually on Fridays, back in the 1950s, five or six freighters belonging to the United States Lines left the New York City docks and headed for northern Europe. There might be the *American Forwarder* going to Dublin, the *American Leader* to Glasgow, the *American Scout* for London, the *American Harvester* to Antwerp and the *American Forester* to Bremerhaven. Usually, they cleared before midnight on Friday so as to escape the high weekend overtime charges. United States Lines were often quite empty on weekends.

These freighters were wartime-built C-2 type design – 7,500 tons and 459ft in length, steam-turbine driven with about 17-knot speeds and, along with five holds of highly profitable cargos, they had space for twelve passengers, comfortably housed in six doubles, each with a bedroom and private shower and toilet. A nine-day fare to, say, Antwerp was set at $150 in 1959.

Vincent Love, who worked in the passenger department of United States Lines, but mostly for the luxury liners *United States* and *America*, had a stint in the late fifties looking after the passengers aboard the freighters:

There were five, six, even seven sailings a week and each ship was full up with 12 passengers. Lots of travellers liked them. They were less fancy than the liners and offered a more casual, relaxed way to and from Europe. Once, one of the freighters broke down outside New York and had to return to the Manhattan Piers. I bought copies of the *Journal American* and that pleased them. They read while the repairs were made.

Miles MacMahon served in the 1950s as a radio officer aboard three of these ships – the *American Scout*, *American Forester* and *American Producer*. He recalled:

> They were classic American freighters of that time, but they were also modified sometimes to suit their trades. The *American Scout*, for example, was specially fitted to go up the Manchester Ship Canal in England. The stack and the masts were on hinges and so could be lowered for bridge clearances. The ships were kept in tip-top condition – they were always immaculate. They used the Chelsea Piers, No. 59 through 62, on Manhattan's West Side. Inbound from Europe, the ship would discharge cargo first at New York and then go off on a seven- to ten-day 'coastal swing' – calling at Boston, Philadelphia, Baltimore, Norfolk and Charleston. Then they would return to New York to finish loading for a return to Europe. All cargo was loaded in pallets and nets. There were no containers then.

Loading cargo: United States Lines' *American Forwarder* taking on cargo at New York's Chelsea Piers. (United States Lines)

Miles MacMahon was quite unique among seamen – he worked part-time, in the summers only, as a ship's radio officer. He was a high school physics teacher in New Jersey for the other nine months. 'I made $5,000 a year teaching in 1960,' he recalled:

> … but made more than that for only three summer voyages on United States Lines. We'd sail to various ports – Hamburg, Bremerhaven, the King George V Docks at London. We also had other, special sailings. On the *American Producer*, I recall once going to western Europe – to St-Nazaire in France and to Bilbao and Santander in Spain. Altogether, there were three-week round-trips on US Lines freighters. We also carried a dozen or so passengers on each ship and, in summer, we had lots of teachers on-board.

When US Lines began adding newer, larger freighters in the early 1960s, passenger quarters were not included. This disappeared after the older ships were retired, many of them finishing up on supply runs to South East Asia during the Vietnam War and then, aged and exhausted, finished their days at Taiwanese scrapyards.

New tonnage for US Lines in the 1960s included the ten ships of the American Challenger class. The 1960s was an era of rebuilding, renewal and improvement for many freighter companies, including American ones.

The sleek 21-knot cargo liner *American Challenger* arrived for a tug and fireboat reception on 28 August 1962. The 11,105grt vessel, with a resemblance to the super liner *United States*, the fastest passenger ship afloat, sailed within three days on her maiden crossing to Le Havre and London. She was the beginning of a new, super-express service for United States Lines that cut two days off the passage of the average freighter. The *Challenger's* record run was between Ambrose Lightship and Bishop Rock in England in four days and twenty-three hours. On her very first eastbound crossing, she averaged 24.42 knots.

United States Lines turned to container shipping in the late 1960s, then built purposeful containerships, but collapsed into bankruptcy in 1986. The United States Lines' name was later briefly resurrected for a small container firm, but on the US West Coast.

Cunard Line

The great Cunard Line, best known for its passenger liners, ran a separate cargo service to New York – from London as well as Liverpool and Glasgow.

Inbound – Heading home to New York: The 459ft-long *American Packer* departs from Liverpool. (Alex Duncan)

Noted American maritime artist Carl Evers painted this view of a collection of US shipping lines represented in this Brooklyn shipyard scene. Included are the Ward Line, Esso, American Export, Isthmian, United Fruit, Moore-McCormack and Farrell. The view dates from 1950. (Author's Collection)

The latter was well known as the 'whisky run' because of its large consignments of whiskies made in Scotland and brought to America. Cunard freighters also carried British-made woollens, bicycles and even racehorses to New York.

Cunard withdrew from conventional freighter service in the late 1960s when the company became a partner in the formation of Atlantic Container Line.

American Export Lines

With a considerable fleet of over two dozen freighters, American Export's cargo ships practically berthed in the author's backyard – at Harborside Terminal at Jersey City until the mid fifties and then at Port Authority Piers A, B and C in Hoboken until 1970. Often, there were several Export freighters at berth at the same time and often they were uniquely berthed, what one captain called 'bow-out, stern-in'. It seems that the company's marine superintendent preferred it that way – it made for easier departures. At Hoboken, Export freighters occasionally berthed at the outer ends of Piers A and C, awaiting an inner, regular berth. Company freighters almost always featured in the daily shipping schedules of the *New York Times* and *Herald Tribune*.

Business for American Export was booming in the 1950s. There were about two dozen freighters in the company fleet, many of them standardised ships, belonging to the 8,500-ton, 459ft-long Exporter class. They each had names beginning with 'Ex' – such as *Express*, *Expeditor*, *Exemplar*, *Exminster* and *Excellency*. Along with lots of freight, many of them carried up to twelve passengers.

There were other ships as well – like *Exton* and *Exmouth*, which were Victory ships from World War Two. A few of these carried up to six passengers, but all in the same cabin and were sold only to male passengers. Export also ran two large, luxurious liners, the 1,000-passenger sister ships *Independence* and *Constitution*, both of which were completed in 1951. The company also had the so-called 'Four Aces', a quartet of passenger-cargo ships that carried 125 first-class travellers and which were named *Excalibur*, *Excambion*, *Exeter* and *Exochorda*.

Spices from the Middle East: American Export's *Examiner* docked stern-first at Hoboken's Pier C. (James McNamara Collection)

Sister ships: *Exhibitor* (left) and *Excellency* undergoing repairs at Bethlehem Steel's Key Highway shipyard at Baltimore. (James McNamara Collection)

Special occasion: the nuclear-powered *Savannah* makes her first call at Rotterdam, 1965. (Nico Guns Collection)

With a fleet of some thirty different ships, all used on the Mediterranean and Middle East runs, it was said that an American Export vessel passed through the Straits of Gibraltar every twenty-four hours. 'The Mediterranean was our primary run, the backbone of the company,' remembered Robert Capello, who worked in both the company's freight as well as passenger departments, both located in their Lower Manhattan offices:

Our long-haul freight service was through the Suez Canal to India, Pakistan, Ceylon and Burma. I remember that, in the 1950s and '60s, we carried lots of rags out to Bombay, but returned with finished clothing. There were also lots of spices and teas going to the States. From the Mediterranean, we brought cans of olive oil and leather goods from Italy, wines from Spain and oranges from Israel. Over to Europe, we transported lots of American-manufactured goods: machinery, automobiles, trucks, locomotives and even household appliances like stoves and refrigerators.

American Export freighters regularly sailed to the likes of Lisbon, Cadiz, Barcelona, Marseilles, Genoa, Tunis, Piraeus, Salonika, Iskenderun, Haifa,

Alexandria, Bombay and Karachi, and typically for freighters of that era, they did the so-called 'East Coast swing', as it was called. While the longest stays were at New York (Hoboken), they also called in for additional cargo at Boston, Philadelphia, Baltimore and Norfolk/Hampton Roads.

In 1960, American Export bought out another US-flag shipping line, the Isbrandtsen Company, and together they now had over forty ships. Noted especially for its eastbound round-the-world service with freighters with 'flying' names, such as *Flying Gull* and *Flying Enterprise*, the two firms were soon renamed (by 1962) as the American Export-Isbrandtsen Lines.

By the mid-1960s, American Export was offering twice-monthly sailings, using the quartet *Export Ambassador*, *Export Adventurer*, *Export Aide* and *Export Agent*, from New York to Lisbon, Casablanca, Tel Aviv, Haifa, Larnaca, Iskenderun, Valencia, Alicante, Malaga, Seville, Cadiz, Portimão and Lisbon. The round-trips took seven weeks. In addition, there were other sailings to Mediterranean ports and the Middle East.

However, by this time there were great changes in shipping as containerisation began. It was now all more efficient and required different, more purposeful vessels. Export was a forerunner and began by converting two bulk carriers to carry up to 660 20ft cargo containers. Soon, Container Transport Lines was a specially created subsidiary and early experimentation even included the loading of containers by helicopter!

The company also dabbled in commercial use of nuclear power by chartering (from the US Government) the world's first nuclear merchant ship, the 14,000-ton, sixty-passenger *Savannah*. They leased this $60 million ship, intended to be a prototype of many, for $1 a year from the Federal Maritime Administration. Export even proposed a fleet of as many as thirty 'nuclear super ships' to strengthen and also revive the already sagging American merchant marine. Sadly, however, the 595ft-long *Savannah* proved to be very expensive as well as difficult to operate. Also, because of the potential risks with her reactor, she was not always welcome in foreign ports. Many harbour officials even insisted, for example, that the ship dock stern-in so as to make a quick, emergency getaway if needed. She sailed for only six years before being made over as a museum ship. Presently (in 2017), after being 'mothballed' for some years near Norfolk, she is waiting in Baltimore, supposedly to be restored as a floating museum, but moored near Washington DC.

American Export also built new break-bulk freighters and then purposeful containerships in the 1960s, but gradually faced declining markets. Less expensive, foreign-flag tonnage was now a big problem. Downsizing, the company left Hoboken in 1970 and relocated to smaller New York Harbor terminal operations at the Bush Terminal in Brooklyn.

In 1978, the company was bought out by another American shipowner, Farrell Lines, and soon lost its identity. In 2000, Farrell itself was bought out by P&O-Nedlloyd, the British-Dutch shipping giant (itself, now owned by Denmark's Maersk Line), and was reduced to but a few ships as the Farrell Mediterranean Express.

One of the last former Export ships, the *Argonaut,* was used on the ammunition run out to Iraq. Another, the *Export Banner,* went to scrap in Texas in 2007. The long-gone, but still wonderful ships of American Export are left these days to the history books.

—⁂—

Freighters Sailing from New York: January 1953

SATURDAY, 24 JANUARY

American Planter	United States Lines	Hamburg
City of Brisbane	Ellerman	Sydney
Noordam	Holland America	Rotterdam
Poelau Laut	Java Pacific	Mid-East ports

SUNDAY, 25 JANUARY

American Counselor	United States Lines	Amsterdam
Alcoa Puritan	Alcoa	Trinidad

MONDAY, 26 JANUARY

American Builder	United States Lines	Liverpool

TUESDAY, 27 JANUARY

Roseville	Barber	Lagos
Exbrook	American Export	Trieste
Villa do Porto	Flomarcy	Funchal
Ganymedes	Royal Netherlands	Trinidad

WEDNESDAY, 28 JANUARY

Ocean Victory	Stockard	Genoa
Pioneer Glen	United States Lines	Brisbane
Kaituna	New Zealand Shipping	Auckland
Quirigua	United Fruit Company	Kingston

THURSDAY, 29 JANUARY

American Clipper	United States Lines	Bremen
American Manufacturer	United States Lines	Liverpool
Robin Sherwood	Robin	Cape Town
Steel Executive	Isthmian	Penang
Steel Vendor	Isthmian	Basrah
Agamemnon	Royal Netherlands	Port-au-Prince
San Jose	United Fruit	Cristóbal
Beatrice	Bull	San Juan

FRIDAY, 30 JANUARY

African Endeavor	Farrell	Cape Town
African Patriot	Farrell	Accra
Exochorda	American Export	Alexandria
Taurus	Barber	Lagos
Atlit	Zim	Haifa
Lindi	Belgian	Lobito
Mormacisle	Moore-McCormack (Mor-Mac)	Oslo
Mormacswan	Mor-Mac	Recife
Mormacyork	Mor-Mac	Santos
Oklahoma	DFDS	Gothenburg
Santa Isabel	Grace	Valparaíso
Santa Sofia	Grace	Barranquilla
Santa Ana	Grace	Cumaná
Alcoa Runner	Alcoa	San Juan
Copan	United Fruit	Puerto Limon
Cape Avinof	United Fruit	Havana
Suzanne	Bull	San Juan
Marine Snapper	Luckenbach	Cristóbal

—⁂—

Five Holland America freighters at berth in Hoboken in this October 1948 view. The liner *Nieuw Amsterdam* is in the centre, at the 5th Street Pier. (Hoboken Historical Museum)

There are five Holland America freighters in this view, dated 7 April 1951, at Rotterdam. Again, the *Nieuw Amsterdam* is in centre position; the twin-funnelled *Volendam* is on the far right. (Nico Guns Collection)

Holland America Line

While often known for its transatlantic passenger liners, ships such as the *Nieuw Amsterdam*, *Statendam* and *Rotterdam*, Holland America also ran a sizeable freighter fleet, typically well-maintained, trim vessels that more often berthed across the Hudson River from New York City, in Hoboken, New Jersey. The local longshoremen, those dockers immortalised in Hollywood's brilliant *On the Waterfront* (filmed along the Hoboken docks and premiered in 1954), referred to them as the 'dyk ships' – vessels such as the *Schiedyk*, *Sloterdayk*, *Sommelsdyk* and *Soestdyk*. The big liners were the 'dam ships' – harbour legends such as the *Nieuw Amsterdam* and *Rotterdam*.

The Fifth Street Pier was the longer and better fitted, and so therefore handled the liners; the adjoining Sixth Street dock was for freighters mostly, the company's separate fleet of smart-looking, always immaculate cargo ships that also often carried up to twelve passengers each.

There were post-war, US-built Victory- and bigger C-3-class ships, which used an 'A' nomenclature. A series of six K-class freighters were added in the mid-1950s and then, bigger still and with engines aft, the G-class of the early sixties. Together, they sailed the North Atlantic, to and from northern Europe, and there were at least two sailings each week in those now distant-days, before the advent of of fast and efficient container ships.

Holland America's *Grotedyk* departs from Rotterdam on a voyage to the Gulf of Mexico ports. (Nico Guns Collection)

Holland America's Atlantic liners sailed between Hoboken, Southampton, Le Havre and Rotterdam; the freighters went to Rotterdam as well, but also to Antwerp, Bremen and Hamburg. Generally, they carried American-made manufactured goods over to Europe and returned with the likes of Dutch cheeses, Dutch tulip bulbs and Dutch beer. There were also occasional notations. Holland America also carried the likes of the very first Volkswagen sent to the United States, which arrived in a wooden crate in 1949 at the Fifth Street Pier on the 12,000-ton *Westerdam*, a passenger-cargo liner.

Holland America also offered a freighter service to southern US ports and Mexico. The author met Captain W.J. Deijnen on a Caribbean cruise in the fall of 2016. The itinerary began at Fort Lauderdale, but finished in New Orleans. Notably, it would be Captain Deijnen's first visit to that Louisiana port in fifty-five years, since he was sailing as a young apprentice officer with the famed Holland America Line on-board one of their freighters:

> My first ship was the *Schiedyk*, a 9,000-ton freighter but which also carried twelve passengers. It had been built by Harland & Wolff at Belfast just after World War Two, in 1948. The original intention was to use that ship [and her sister ship, the *Soestdyk*] on the affiliate Java–New York Line, sailing between New York and the former Dutch East Indies. Instead, by 1954, the *Schiedyk* was sailing between northern Europe [Bremen, Rotterdam, Antwerp, etc] and ports in the Gulf of Mexico [New Orleans, Mobile, Galveston, Veracruz, etc.]. The *Schiedyk* and her sister were built in Northern Ireland, at Belfast, because Holland America was owed some steel dating from World War One. The *Statendam III* was built there, but requisitioned by the British [used as the troopship *Justicia*] for trooping and later sunk. Holland America was allocated reparation, mostly in steel. Building the *Schiedyk* was part of that compensation.
>
> One of my fellow crew members on the *Schiedyk* was rather famous. A greaser on-board, he was one of only three who survived the World War Two sinking of the *Zaandam* [also Holland America Line] but then endured eighty-three days in a lifeboat before being rescued. It remains a record to this day.

'Westbound to the States, Holland America cargo ships carried tulips, caraway seeds, agricultural products, cheeses and lots of Heineken beer,' remembered the late Captain Cornelius van Herk, who served aboard about a dozen company freighters in the late 1940s and 1950s:

> Going back to Holland, we carried American-manufactured goods, machinery, tin plate and lots of grain that was loaded by floating elevators. We later expanded this service [in August 1949] to Germany, to Bremen and Hamburg. These were our first German calls since before the War.

Swedish American Line

The author remembers the Swedish American freighters as always looking immaculate – in full white and with their distinctive funnel markings of three gold crowns on a blue disc. Based in Gothenburg and part of the Broström Group, Swedish American ran ten-day crossings between New York and Gothenburg. In addition to freight, their ships offered up to

French Line's *Suffren* is loading for a voyage to Le Havre. The same terminal in Red Hook, Brooklyn, was rebuilt in 2005 for use by the Cunard Line and the *Queen Mary 2*. (Port Authority of New York & New Jersey)

twelve berths for passengers. I recall often seeing the *Stureholm*, a handsome, always immaculate freighter, which sometimes used Manhattan's Pier 97, normally the berth used by Swedish American's splendid passenger liners.

American Scantic Line

An arm of the South American-routed Moore-McCormack (or Mor-Mac) Lines, American Scantic offered a weekly North Atlantic service between New York and other US East Coast ports to Oslo, Gothenburg and Copenhagen. Mor-Mac tended to use slightly larger, perhaps sturdier, freighters on this route – ships such as the 7,900grt 492ft-long *Mormacsaga*, *Mormacisle* and *Mormacpenn*.

States Marine Lines

The States Marine Lines named their ships after the nicknames of American states. They ran services to northern Europe, the Mediterranean and 'round-the-world'.

Black Diamond Line

Also known for their Friday departures from New York, Black Diamond used Norwegian-flag freighters that carried considerable cargo and up to twelve passengers. The company serviced northern Europe – crossing to Antwerp, Rotterdam, Amsterdam, Hamburg and Bremen. Owned by Sigurd Herlofson & Co., their ships all had a 'Black' prefix to the names and were named after birds: *Black Eagle*, *Black Falcon*, *Black Hawk*, *Black Heron*, *Black Osprey*, *Black Swan* and *Black Tern*.

Lykes Line

This large American firm, based at New Orleans, had a very large fleet in the 1950s and 1960s. Named after family members of the original founding Lykes brothers, they offered worldwide services including from the US Gulf to Europe.

Founded in 1900, Lykes Brothers went into shipping in 1922 and, by the 1960s, had a fleet of fifty-four vessels. Although they made the transition into containerised shipping, the company filed for bankruptcy in 1995 and was soon sold to CP Ships. The Lykes brand was retained for another decade, until 2005, and then was dropped. A year later, CP Ships and the last remains of Lykes were bought by Germany's TUI AG and merged into their Hapag-Lloyd division.

Meyer Line

I well remember the Meyer Line from New York Harbor, from its pier at the north end of the Brooklyn waterfront, located at the foot of Joralemon Street. Often, there were two of their sturdy, handsome, always immaculately kept ships at berth. One was inbound from northern Europe and was about to go off on a quick, ten-day round of other US East Coast ports (Boston, Philadelphia, Baltimore and Norfolk) while the other was taking on its final loads of freight before heading back into North Atlantic waters. Usually, the outbound sailing was fixed for a Friday afternoon, just before the to-be-avoided-at-all-costs high weekend overtime charges went into effect on those then busy, highly unionised New York docks.

Meyer Line's smart-looking *Havjo* berthed in Brooklyn on a winter's day in 1966. (Gillespie-Faber Collection)

The upper Brooklyn docks in a view, dated 1968, which includes the Meyer Line terminal. (Author's Collection)

Meyer had a large tanker fleet as well. The freighters on the New York run were often quite large for the time, often over 10,000 tons, and they usually had a vast collection of masts and booms to handle their cargos. Meyer used a 'Hav' nomenclature and so their grey-hulled ships had names such as *Havjo*, *Havhok*, *Havmann* and *Havprins*. A large, white 'M' was displayed on their funnels as well as on the tips of their bows.

Represented in the United States by the Lower Manhattan offices of one of the then great shipping agents, Boyd, Weir & Sewell, the Meyer Line had weekly sailings to Antwerp, Hamburg and/or Bremen. Rotterdam and Le Havre were sometimes included as well.

The passenger quarters on the Meyer Line ships, for twelve guests or less, were said to be very comfortable and included a small dining room (shared with the officers), a lounge with soft chairs and sofas, and single as well as double cabins. Fares in the 1960s were $210 to Holland or Germany in winter and $235 in peak summer. Meyer had a strong and loyal following, including businessmen who wanted a rest during an ocean crossing, government personnel and their families being reassigned overseas and travellers who disliked the big, fancier passenger-filled ocean liners. In the freighter-passenger trades to northern Europe, Meyer competed directly with the likes of the Belgian Line, United States Lines, Holland America Line, Black Diamond Line and the Cosmopolitan Line, which was also Norwegian-owned.

Meyer began to carry some of the more efficient cargo containers, which were stowed on the open outer decks, by the late 1960s and even relocated to more spacious loading facilities over in Port Newark, New Jersey. They did not, however, follow the likes of Cunard, the French Line, Holland America and Swedish American by investing in large containership consortiums. Instead, by 1972 they were gone completely from transatlantic freighter service and consequently so was their interest in carrying four to twelve passengers aboard their ships. Eventually, Meyer pulled out of the tanker and tramp-charter trades as well. The business of shipping had been through a virtual revolution with the coming of the container age and, rather sadly, the Meyer Line was lost in the shuffle.

Oranje Line

This Dutch company offered transatlantic services out of Rotterdam, Southampton and Le Havre to the St Lawrence region, Montreal and Quebec City, and (following the opening of the St Lawrence Seaway in

Meyer was a well-known name in shipping circles back in the 1950s and 1960s, but it was not German as many thought. It was in fact a Norwegian firm, P. Meyer & Company, based in Oslo, but which rarely traded to Norwegian ports.

1959) to Great Lakes ports including Toronto and Chicago. In winter, when the St Lawrence was closed, the service terminated at Halifax and Saint John. Due to limitations of the seaway, Oranje Line used smaller ships – such as the 2,300-ton freighters *Prins Alexander* and *Prins Johan Willem Friso*.

Manchester Liners

This firm, with headquarters in Manchester, England, ran two Atlantic services: weekly between Manchester and Montreal (or Saint John in winter) and bi-monthly between Manchester and US East Coast ports (New York, Baltimore, Norfolk, Charleston and Jacksonville).

Thordén Line

Swedish-flag Thordén Line was also part of what one harbour photographer dubbed, 'the Friday armada' – ships departing by Friday evening to avoid the hefty weekend overtime along New York's waterfront. Smart-looking if smaller freighters, the regulars had family names and included the *Selma Thordén, Clary Thordén* and *Hjordis Thordén,* which made weekly crossings to Gothenburg, Oslo and Copenhagen.

The Belgian Line Piers Nos 14 and 15, in Lower Manhattan. (Author's Collection)

Finnlines

In the 1960s, Finnlines operated break-bulk freighters between New York, Hamburg, Helsinki and Turku or Kotka, among other routes.

Belgian Line

The Compagnie Maritime Belge – or the Belgian Line as it was known in the US – ran two services. One, using Victory-class ships such as the *Vnkt, Lindi* and *Burckel,* was a direct New York–Antwerp route. The other, often referred to as the Belgian-African Line, ran a service between New York, St Vincent in the Cape Verde Islands to Matadi (fifteen days from New York), Luanda and Lobito.

Cosmopolitan Line

Norwegian shipowner A/S J. Ludwig Mowinckels Rederi traded to New York as the Cosmopolitan Line. Their smart-looking ships – with names such as *Horda, Ronda, Lista* and *Heina* – offered weekly sailings, mostly on Fridays, from Manhattan's Pier 56. Also calling at other US East Coast ports, they were routed on the North Atlantic to Le Havre, Antwerp and Rotterdam. Cosmopolitan was among those companies that faded in the mid-1960s era of containerisation.

Norwegian America Line

Oslo-based and well known for its passenger liners, Norwegian America also ran a regular freighter service between New York, other US ports, Oslo and other ports in Norway.

Special occasion: Spanish Line's *Guadalupe* arriving in New York on her maiden voyage in 1953. (James McNamara Collection)

Norwegian America's *Tyrifjord* berthed at Oslo, with the liner *Sagafjord* behind. (ALF Collection)

The harbour at Gothenburg, Sweden, with the passenger ship *Saga* in the foreground. (Author's Collection)

Spanish Line – Compañía Transatlántica Española

In the 1950s, Pier 15 at the foot of Maiden Lane was the New York home of the Spanish Line and their twin passenger-cargo ships, the 10,200-ton *Covadonga* and *Guadalupe*. Built in the early 1950s in Spain, they were comparatively small ships but carried up to 350 passengers each in two classes, first and second. They traded across the mid Atlantic to and from a collection of Spanish ports but then, after calling at New York, made extended sailings to the Caribbean, stopping at Havana (replaced by San Juan after Castro arrived in 1959–60) and Vera Cruz.

The 487ft-long *Covadonga* and *Guadalupe* visited New York every two weeks and then remained in port for four or five days, offloading and then loading cargo. They would deliver the likes of coffee from the Caribbean, wines and olives from Spain and, on outward trips, took on American-manufactured goods.

Their trade inevitably fell away and by the late 1960s, both ships were downgraded to freighter status, limited only to twelve passengers each.

Prudential Lines

New York-based Prudential Lines used Victory ships on its transatlantic freighter trade. Each Friday, ships such as the 7,600grt 17-knot *Newberry Victory* cast off for ports in the Mediterranean – to the likes of Casablanca, Barcelona, Genoa, Naples and Piraeus.

Costa Line

Another firm best known for its passenger ships, until the 1970s, Genoa-based Costa Line (Giacomo Costa fu Andrea) ran freighters between New York, Genoa and other ports along the west coast of Italy. Initially using second-hand ships – surplus American-built Liberty ships and others acquired from the likes of Canadian Pacific and Maersk Line – the company added, in 1958, two rather notable large freighters, the 13,200-ton *Maria Costa* and *Pia Costa*. With engines-aft design, they measured 551ft in length.

Hellenic Lines

'Hellenic built a large fleet that began with older, pre-war freighters as well as American surplus Liberty ships for its US East and Gulf Coast–Mediterranean–Middle East service. New tonnage began in the sixties,' noted Captain James McNamara.

Hellenic services were quite extensive. The mainline Mediterranean route, with two sailings per month, traded between the US East Coast and Genoa, Naples, Piraeus, Salonika, Istanbul, Lattakia, Izmir and Iskenderun. The extended Persian Gulf run, also with twice-monthly sailings from the US East Coast, was generally routed to Alexandria, Beirut, Jeddah, Port Sudan, Basrah, Khorramshahr, Kuwait, Dammam, Bahrain, Umm Said, Karachi, Bombay, Madras, Rangoon, Chittagong, and turnaround at Calcutta.

Carrying up to twelve passengers on most ships, the Mediterranean itinerary was offered for one-way passages, but also as a full fifty to sixty-five-day cruise (from $650 per person in 1960); the Persian Gulf itinerary, lasting seventy-five to ninety days was priced from $825.

Captain McNamara recalls:

Hellenic carried lots of jute and burlap as their main cargo on homeward voyages from India. But similar to other Greek families in the shipping business when Pericles Callimanopulos, owner of Hellenic Lines, died in the early 1980s, his sons fought over the company. Furthermore, after the fall of the Shah of Iran in 1979, US trade to Iran collapsed. Then big, US oil companies pulled out and the shipping trade, especially of oil-related machinery, all but vanished. This spelled the end for Hellenic Lines as well as others like the German-flag Hansa Line.

Khedivial Mail Line

In the 1950s, this was the only Egyptian-flag company running a regular service across the Atlantic, between Alexandria, several other Mediterranean ports and New York, as well as US coastal ports. The service was later extended to go beyond Suez, to Karachi and Bombay. The company's prime ships were two converted, American-built Victory ships, the *Khedive Ismail* (later renamed *Cleopatra*) and *Mohammed Ali El-Kebir*. They crossed westbound with lots of Egyptian textiles (and later teas, spices and more textiles from India) and returned with American-manufactured goods. As refitted ships, the pair earned income: each ship also had quarters for up to seventy-five passengers each.

Zim Lines

Following Israeli independence in 1948, Zim ran older, if not quite elderly, ships on the Haifa–New York run. However, by the mid-1950s and because of post-war West German reparations, two fine combination passenger-cargo ships, the 9,900grt *Israel* and *Zion*, greatly enhanced the service. In addition to cargo in five holds, both carried as many as 313 passengers in two-class quarters.

Bound for Haifa: heavy goods being loaded at Brooklyn's Kent Street Pier aboard Zim Lines' *Israel*. (Gillespie-Faber Collection)

Turkish Maritime Lines

This Istanbul-based firm operated worldwide services including US East Coast ports to/from Genoa, Marseilles, Naples, Piraeus and Istanbul.

Jugolinija

Based at Rijeka and crossing over to New York and other US East Coast ports, older – and sometimes very old – freighters maintained service. They were assisted by a Victory ship, refitted as the *Hrvatska*, and a former German freighter, the *Srbija*. Both had adequate cargo space for their sailings from Rijeka, Trieste, Naples and Casablanca. They also carried passengers – sixty on-board the *Hrvatska* and forty-four on the *Srbija*.

'Jugolinija had mostly second-hand ships in the 1950s, but then began to build new tonnage,' recalled Captain James McNamara. 'Their new ships were quite lovely and very modern for their time. Jugolinija lasted into the container age, but then was dispersed following the break-up of Yugoslavia.'

Similarly, another Yugoslavian firm, Splosna Plovba, also offered Atlantic service.

When completed, the 11,185grt *American Courier* ranked as one of the fastest freighters in the world. (Author's Collection)

The Liverpool Docks: the C2-class freighters *American Producer* and *American Scout*. (Author's Collection)

Waiting on a Saturday afternoon: American Export's 473ft-long *Express* at Pier C, Hoboken, in September 1966. (Author's Collection)

The *Flying Eagle* being worked by a heavy-lift crane at Pier A, Hoboken. (Norman Knebel Collection)

The sleek, 595ft-long *Savannah*, America's bid to use nuclear power for commercial shipping. (ALF Collection)

Built in 1944, the Victory ship *Amsteldyk* of the Holland America Line, in the Thames. (Kenneth Wrightman, courtesy of Mick Lindsay)

The combination passenger-cargo liner *Westerdam*, which carried freight on the Rotterdam–New York run. (ALF Collection)

Loading at Rotterdam: Holland America's *Gorredyk* loading cargo. (Holland America Line)

Along the Hudson: the Belgian Line Piers Nos 14 and 15, in Lower Manhattan in 1962. (ALF Collection)

Completed in 1963, the 491ft-long *Aimee Lykes* at Durban. (Mick Lindsay Collection)

Jugolinija's *Zvir*, used on the Rijeka–Mediterranean–New York route, could also carry up to fifty passengers. (Mick Lindsay Collection)

A big, fast Mariner-class freighter, the *Iberville* of Waterman Steamship Co. rests at the Todd Shipyard in Hoboken, New Jersey. (Norman Knebel Collection)

Clockwise from *top left*:

The heavy-lift floating crane *Century* loads cargo at Port Newark, New Jersey. (James McNamara Collection)

United Fruit's handsome *Talamanca* at Pier 3, in Lower Manhattan with the excursion steamer *Sandy Hook* just behind. (Gillespie-Faber Collection)

Another United Fruit vessel: the 100-passenger *Jamaica* at New Orleans between voyages to Central America. (Mick Lindsay Collection)

Banana boat: the smart-looking *Tenadores* berthed at Cristóbal. (Mick Lindsay Collection)

High and dry: Bull Line's *Jean* in dry dock at the Todd Shipyard, Hoboken. (Norman Knebel Collection)

Trading to tropical waters: the combination passenger-cargo ship *Camito* berthed at the Empress Dock, Southampton. Along with cargo, especially homeward-bound bananas, the 8,867grt ship also had quarters for over 100 passengers. (Mick Lindsay Collection)

Misty setting: a superb painting of Royal Mail Lines' *Loch Loyal* by Bermuda-based maritime artist Stephen Card. (Stephen Card)

Via Panama: used on the UK–North American Pacific run, the *Pacific Stronghold* is seen berthed at Vancouver. (Mick Lindsay Collection)

Anti-clockwise from *left*:

In an evocative view at Bermuda, the *Cotopaxi* of PSNC, the Pacific Steam Navigation Co. (Stephen Card)

Big loads: Harrison Line's *Adventurer*, built in 1960, had its own heavy-lift equipment. She is seen at Lourenço Marques in May 1965. (Mick Lindsay Collection)

Dating from 1955, the 8,367-ton *Defender* is seen berthed at Liverpool in September 1969. (Mick Lindsay Collection)

Engines-aft design: the 493ft-long *Inventor* of Harrison Line also had heavy-lift equipment. (Mick Lindsay Collection)

Skilful handling: Harrison's *Journalist* coming into Avonmouth stern first and under the care of the tug *Sea Volunteer*. (Mick Lindsay Collection)

Booth Line's combination passenger-cargo ship *Hubert* berthed along the Amazon at Manaus. (Mick Lindsay Collection)

Clockwise from *top left*:

Power at sea: another superb painting by Stephen Card of Blue Star's *Hobart Star*. (Stephen Card Collection)

Wool from Australia: the 573ft *Auckland Star*, dating from 1958, loading in the London Docks. (Mick Lindsay Collection)

The classic 1935-built *Brisbane Star* berthed at Southampton's Western Docks with the *Queen Elizabeth* and *Athlone Castle* behind. (Kenneth Wrightman Collection, courtesy of Mick Lindsay)

The 1945-built *California Star* passing through the Panama Canal in August 1967. (Mick Lindsay Collection)

Distinctive funnels: the 10,657grt *Queensland Star* inside the King George V Dock in London. (Mick Lindsay Collection)

Skilful handling: the combination passenger-cargo liner *Paraguay Star* in the lock between the Victoria and Royal Albert Docks, London. (Mick Lindsay Collection)

With heavy-lift equipment, *Timaru Star* represented a new generation of Blue Star freighters of the late 1960s. (Mick Lindsay Collection)

Maintenance: *Rockhampton Star* in dry dock at Southampton. The *QE2* is seen on the left. The date is August 1969. (Mick Lindsay Collection)

Classic lines: Hamburg Sud's *Cap San Diego*, built in 1962, later became a museum in Hamburg. (ALF Collection)

ELMA Lines' *Rio Calincasta* berthed in Brooklyn Heights, New York, in 1973. (Author's Collection)

Inbound in New York's Lower Bay, Farrell Lines' *African Planet* heads for her berth at 33rd Street in Brooklyn. (Norman Knebel Collection)

Afternoon arrival: the imposing *African Mercury* returns to New York from a two-month-long voyage to South and East Africa. (Norman Knebel Collection)

Soon sailing for South and East African ports, the beautiful *City of Port Elizabeth* – with accommodation for up to 107 passengers – pauses at the Tilbury Landing Stage to collect her guests. (Kenneth Wrightman Collection, courtesy of Mick Lindsay)

Ellerman's *City of Poona* outbound in Holland's New Waterway. (Mick Lindsay Collection)

Outward bound: on a bright, sunny morning, *City of Adelaide* has a gentle roll. (Mick Lindsay Collection)

City of Adelaide sails through loose pack ice in May 1971. (Mick Lindsay Collection)

The classic-looking *City of Birmingham* departs from Birkenhead. (Kenneth Wrightman, Mick Lindsay Collection)

The great Port of London: the veteran *City of Kimberley* entering the Royal Docks. (Kenneth Wrightman, Mick Lindsay Collection)

With her large funnel, the 507ft-long *City of Ripon* was commissioned in 1956. (Dave Vincent, Mick Lindsay Collection)

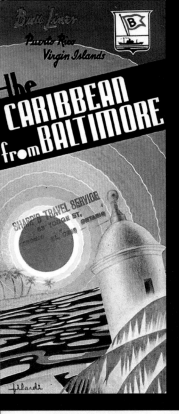

Bull Liner
Puerto Rico
Virgin Islands

the CARIBBEAN from BALTIMORE

Columbus Line

SEA-TRIPS
VIAGENS MARÍTIMAS
VIAJES POR MAR

HWAL

Tarif de passage

HOLLAND WEST - AFRIKA LIJN
SERVICE COMBINÉ
N.V. VEREENIGDE NEDERLANDSCHE SCHEEPVAART MIJ.   N.V. HOLLANDSCHE STOOMBOOT MIJ.

ACROSS THE PACIFIC on the

KLAVENESS LINE ASIATIC SERVICE

PACIFIC COAST
SHANGHAI
HONG KONG
SINGAPORE
JAVA PORTS
CELEBES
BORNEO
PHILIPPINES
HONG KONG
PACIFIC COAST

FOR COMPLETE INFORMATION CONTACT
LYKES BROS. STEAMSHIP CO., INC.
OFFICES AND AGENTS IN PRINCIPAL WORLD PORTS

LYKES LINES
PASSENGER SERVICE
TO AND FROM
- THE UNITED KINGDOM
- THE CONTINENT
- THE MEDITERRANEAN
- THE ORIENT • AFRICA
- THE CARIBBEAN

All Vessels of Lykes Bros. Steamship Co., Inc., are Owned, Registered, Operated, and Built Under the American Flag.

Travel in Informal Comfort

LYKES BROS. STEAMSHIP CO., INC.

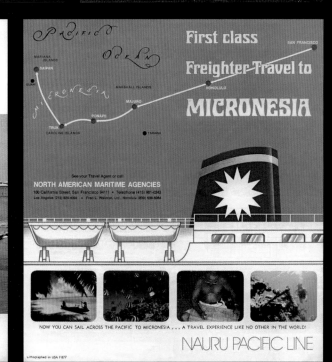

First class
Freighter Travel to
MICRONESIA

See your Travel Agent or call
NORTH AMERICAN MARITIME AGENCIES
100 California Street, San Francisco 94111 • Telephone (415) 981-0343
Los Angeles (213) 624-6394 • Fred L. Waloran, Ltd., Honolulu (808) 538-6084

NOW YOU CAN SAIL ACROSS THE PACIFIC TO MICRONESIA . . . A TRAVEL EXPERIENCE LIKE NO OTHER IN THE WORLD!

NAURU PACIFIC LINE

AMERICAN PRESIDENT LINES
CARGOLINER ADVENTURE CRUISES

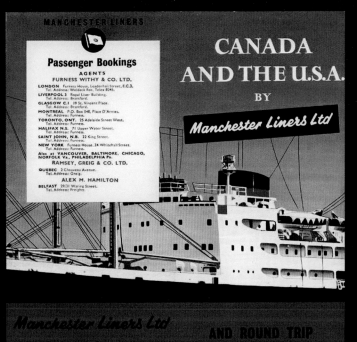

Assorted freighter brochures, etc.
(Author's Collection)

British India's *Nyanza* approaching the Royal Docks in August 1963. (Kenneth Wrightman, Mick Lindsay Collection)

Wartime design: Isthmian's 1945-built *Steel Worker* is between voyages to the Middle East and is berthed at Philadelphia. (Norman Knebel Collection)

2

Sugar and Bananas from the Caribbean

United Fruit Company

While all United Fruit ships had Central American and Caribbean names, the *Junior* was named after the chairman's son – killed in World War Two, he was affectionately called Junior.

In the mid-1950s, business for the United Fruit Company, sometimes referred to as 'Fruitco' and dubbed 'the Great White Fleet', was booming. The company had fifty-five ships that carried 41 million stems of bananas each year, many of these into New York Harbor.

United Fruit had three to four departures each week. Ships such as the 7,200-ton *Esparta* would arrive from Caribbean and Central American ports and then tie-up at United Fruit's specially built (in 1950) 'banana exchange' terminal along the Hudson River in Weehawken, New Jersey. The bananas would be offloaded by special conveyor cranes and transferred to refrigerated railway freight cars and freezer-cooled trucks. Once fully unloaded, the 459ft-long *Esparta* would then be 'shifted' to the company's Lower Manhattan Piers for reloading, but with general cargo.

At the age of 25 and with rising operational costs, many American freighters were either retired or sold to foreign owners. The *Esparta*, which was first commissioned in September 1945, was transferred in 1970 to a United Fruit affiliate, Elders & Fyffes Ltd, and placed under the British flag in 1970. She was renamed *Toloa*, sailed for another seven years and then was sold to scrappers in Taiwan. Her career spanned thirty-three years.

United Fruit itself went through many changes in more recent years. After dropping its US-flag registry in 1971 it instead took on foreign-flag charter tonnage. In the wake of serious financial problems during the 1970s, United Fruit was bought out in 1984 and renamed Chiquita Brands International.

Going bananas: the banana-offloading terminal at Weehawken, New Jersey, with the *Esparta* arriving (left) and the smaller *Cibao* at berth. (United Fruit Company)

Friday afternoon sailing: the *Santa Ana* departs, bound for the Caribbean and Venezuela. (James McNamara Collection)

Standard Fruit Company

Based in New Orleans, but often using chartered foreign-flag tonnage – white-hulled 'banana boats' – Standard Fruit operated four tropical services, including a Central American service with separate runs from New Orleans, as well as New York to La Ceiba in Honduras. Then there was a South American service, also with separate sailings from New Orleans and New York to Guayaquil and Puerto Bolivar in Ecuador. While chartered, the funnels of most Standard Fruit ships bore a 'V' on their funnels; this was for 'Vaccaro', the founders, owning family and long-time managers of Standard Fruit. In more recent times, Standard Fruit has operated under the name Dole Carriers.

Grace Line

The author recalls an occasion in 1963 when no fewer than nine Grace Line ships were moored close to one another. It was during an American seamen's strike and the ships, with voyages cancelled and only light maintenance crews to look after them, were silent and idle. There were the passenger–cargo

Far right: Home from tropical waters: Grace Line's *Santa Rita* makes a late-afternoon arrival on a winter's day. (Grace Line)

Right: Heavily loaded and bound for South America, Grace Line's Santa Cecilia heads from New York for ports along the west coast of South America. In addition to cargo, the 459ft-long ship could carry up to fifty-two passengers in very comfortable quarters. (James McNamara Collection)

The *Santa Teresa* loading at Grace Line's Java Street Pier in Brooklyn. (James McNamara Collection)

Spanking new: the 9,300grt *Santa Lucia* arrives off Lower Manhattan on her maiden call to New York in 1966. The 560ft-long ship could make 20 knots and carry twelve passengers. (James McNamara Collection)

liners *Santa Rosa* and *Santa Paula*, but also five of the Santa Sofia class, smaller passenger-cargo ships that carried up to fifty-two first-class passengers. The ships were together at the Bethlehem Steel Shipyard in Hoboken and also at the adjoining Todd Shipyard. It was perhaps the greatest gathering of Grace Line tonnage at one time.

Grace was one of the best-known companies in the American merchant marine (with some twenty-six ships in 1964), but also in the Latin American trade. Their range of services from both the US east and west coasts encompassed the Caribbean and the west coast of South America.

Alcoa Line

Owned by the Aluminum Company of America, Alcoa Line freighters carried up to twelve passengers in its West Indies and South America service from New York. The 6,500grt *Alcoa Pilgrim* class were assigned to the South American run, usually departing from New York for La Guairá, Puerto Cabello, Guanta, Trinidad, Georgetown, Surinam and Trinidad. Including a return to a US East Coast port, this itinerary was timed to twenty-seven days.

Back in the ship-busy 1950s in New York, the port area in Weehawken, New Jersey, was known primarily for its railways. The old New York Central Railroad controlled a good part of that waterfront from 32nd to 60th Streets. There were huge freight yards, machine and repair shops, piers for tugs and others for barges (both covered and open) and even for ferries (that crossed to Manhattan's West 42nd Street until 1957) and a special dock with two sturdy cranes that handled bigger, bulkier cargos. There was even a huge grain elevator, itself something of a landmark on the western shore of the Hudson. (It was finally pulled down in 1964.) Occasionally, deep-sea freighters came to call. They were usually worked by steam-powered floating derricks known locally as 'goose-neck cranes'. These cranes worked with buckets. The ships were often offloading bauxite that had come up from Trinidad and Surinam. Often, it came aboard the fine-looking freighters of the Alcoa Line or from chartered ships, often flying Scandinavian colours.

Alcoa was a fascinating company back in the fifties. Back in earlier times, well before World War Two, they were known as the Aluminum Line. They were and remained an arm of the giant Aluminum Company of America and thus the subsequent name Alcoa. Their ships were often painted as a product reminder with lots of silver colouring. By the 1950s, they had amassed a good-sized fleet of freighters, mostly 6,800-ton C1-class ships that had five holds and carried up to twelve passengers. They had names grouped by the

Above: Heading for the Caribbean, the *Alcoa Pilgrim* is well loaded. (James McNamara Collection)

Above: Alcoa ships often offloaded cargos at the New York Central Railroad properties in Weehawken, New Jersey. (Author's Collection)

Left: A Spanish freighter offloads sugar at the Domino plant in Baltimore. (Author's Collection)

letter 'P' – *Alcoa Puritan*, *Alcoa Pegasus* and *Alcoa Pointer*. They also had some larger, C2-class ships, that used an 'R' nomenclature. These included the *Alcoa Ranger* and *Alcoa Roamer*.

Alcoa freighters sailed from Weehawken, Lower Manhattan, then Brooklyn and finally Port Newark (then a fledgling, pre-container marine facility in New Jersey) as well as from Philadelphia and Baltimore on sixteen- to twenty-one-day itineraries. One service went to San Juan, Mayaguez and Ponce, while the other called at San Juan, Ponce, St Thomas and St Croix. The larger C2-class were used in the Puerto Rico and Virgin Islands trade – sailing from New York to San Juan, Mayaguez, Ponce, St Thomas, St Croix and a sugar port in Puerto Rico. This itinerary was timed to eighteen-day round-trip.

Alcoa's chartered ships, bearing such names as *Bellavia*, *Maakefjell* and *Rikke Skou*, were generally used on the more extended, thirty-day round-trip service to Venezuela, Trinidad and Surinam. These were called the 'long cruises' and sailed from New York as well as Baltimore. Ports of call included the likes of La Guairá, Puerto Cabello, Maracaibo, Guanta, Paramaribo, Puranam and Moengo. Curaçao and Aruba were sometimes added as well.

Alcoa also ran freighters from Mobile and New Orleans, but increasingly relied on chartered, less expensive, foreign-flag tonnage. They also began offering trips on ore carriers, larger vessels that sometimes carried as few as four passengers. But like many US-flag operators, Alcoa turned fully to freight in the 1970s.

Today, the Weehawken waterfront has been totally rebuilt and gentrified with a bustling ferry service to and from Manhattan, restaurants, sports facilities and lots of luxury housing. Near the very site where Alcoa freighters once berthed, newly constructed riverside town houses were selling (in 2013) for $1 million and up.

Bull Line

This American firm offered sailings between the US East Coast, Puerto Rico and other Caribbean ports. Their ships – with female names such as *Frances*, *Catherine* and *Jean* – also carried six to twelve passengers.

Fyffes Line

Elders & Fyffes Limited, also known as the Fyffes Line, was noted for their smart-looking all-white 'banana boats'. Still trading today but now using chartered tonnage, the earlier British-flag ships of Fyffes had an added romance about them – they sailed to the exotic islands of the Caribbean. They carried UK-manufactured goods outbound and, expectedly, returned often with large loads of bananas – sometimes over 100,000 bunches. By the 1960s, their freighters also carried up to the customary twelve passengers; their two passenger-cargo liners, the *Golfito* and *Camito*, had accommodations for as many as 100.

In the 1960s, Alan Hulse sailed as crew with Fyffes:

I sailed aboard the Fyffes freighters, some of which were quite fast. We'd cross over to Barbados, Trinidad, Grenada and then to Jamaica, to Kingston and Port Antonio. Homeward, sometimes we'd land at Southampton or sometimes at Avonmouth. The port was selected by which one had the best rates for offloading the bananas. Our big competitor in those days was another British company, the Geest Line.

'Fyffes was a very nice company to work for,' added Hulse:

Myself, I was a young seaman struck with wanderlust. Coming from Liverpool, I wanted to see new places. The routes on Fyffes seemed exotic – palm trees, sandy beaches, lots of sun. We often carried up to twelve passengers, mostly older, retired types in winter and who took the entire six-week round-trips. They escaped at least part of the cold, dreary winters in England. But once, I remember we had only two passengers aboard, a honeymoon couple. They had the ship to themselves, but we rarely saw them. Afterward, my next stop was to see South America so I joined another British shipping line, Pacific Steam Navigation Company, which sailed from the UK to the Caribbean as well, but then passed through the Panama Canal and touched on ports all along the west coast of South America as far south as Valparaíso.

Royal Netherlands Steamship Co.

With a large fleet of mostly smaller cargo ships, Holland's KNSM, better known as the Royal Netherlands Steamship Company, had as many as ten sailings per month to the Caribbean and South America from their terminal at 31st Street in Brooklyn. Ships such as the 4,000grt *Adonis*, which could carry up to twelve passengers, was used in a weekly service to Curaçao, Aruba, La Guairá, Puerto Cabello, Maracaibo and Trinidad. Another weekly run was to Port au Prince and Ciudad Trujillo. An alternate, but less regular,

A Royal Netherlands freighter loading at Curaçao. (Author's Collection)

Royal Netherlands freighters loading at Amsterdam. (Royal Netherlands Steamship Co.)

service was to Dutch Guiana and still another to Cap Haïtien and Haitian out ports.

'In the 1950s and '60s, Holland America Line represented the passenger business of other Dutch steamship companies through their network of branch offices in the USA and Canada,' recalled Laurens van der Laan, then employed by Holland America Line:

We had a department at Holland America in New York called Dutch World Services with a staff of seven. I handled KNSM, Royal Netherlands, with their passenger service between New York and the Dutch West Indies. These ships sailed weekly from Brooklyn. So every Thursday and Friday, I took the subway to the 31st Street Pier to attend the embarkation of passengers heading for Curaçao, Aruba, ports in Venezuela and Georgetown in British Guiana and Paramaribo in Dutch Guiana. The ships were very popular and usually quite full.

Rotterdam South America Line

Owned by Holland's Van Nievelt, Goudriaan & Co., this company served the north Europe–east coast of South America route.

Royal Mail Lines

In the mid-1950s, Des Kirkpatrick worked at the Manchester Ship Canal and became fascinated by ships, their flags, owners and especially their overseas ports of call. He remembered:

> I used to take walks during lunchtime and also after work around the docks. I saw all sorts of ships, coming from all over the world. It was all very fascinating – and rather quickly I thought of going to sea. I wrote to and applied to several shipping lines and Royal Mail Lines was the first to reply. They brought me to London, to their offices along Leadenhall Street, for an interview. I was quickly hired, in April 1956, and assigned to the *Gascony*, a freighter that was the second oldest ship in the fleet. The *Gascony* was on Royal Mail's Caribbean run – from the UK to Bermuda, Nassau, the Dominican Republic and then Kingston, Jamaica. We also called at small Jamaican 'out ports' at places like Falmouth and Montego Bay. We'd anchor out and were loaded with rum and bulk sugar by lighters. The rum came in large barrels, which were loaded four or five at a time. Once, a barrel dropped and smashed on deck and the entire ship smelled of rum.

Later, Des was assigned to Royal Mail's other freighters, some of which carried up to twelve passengers:

> I sailed on the *Parima*, *Pilcomayo*, *Loch Garth*, *Ebro* and *Paraguay*. I also did several trips on chartered ships including one flying the Swiss flag and registered at Basel. Then I was transferred to a more luxurious, more comfortable way of life at sea – to the flagship *Andes* and one of the finest liners of her day.

Harrison Line

Britain's Harrison Line had strong interests in the UK–West Indies/Central America service, but also served South Africa and the Middle East. Dating from 1853, the company is possibly best remembered for its naming policy, using professions – ships' names such as *Adventurer*, *Journalist* and *Wayfarer*. They continued to operate a Liverpool–West Indies service until the 1990s, but had ceased trading as a shipowner altogether by 2000.

Pacific Steam Navigation Co. Ltd

Commonly known as PSNC, this long-standing British shipping line traded from British ports to Bermuda, the Bahamas, the Caribbean and, most importantly, to ports along the west coast of South America as far south as Chile. Normally using the Panama route, their ships occasionally returned via the Straits of Magellan.

3

Bags of Coffee: Latin America

Moore-McCormack Lines

Moore-McCormack, commonly referred to as Mor-Mac, was primarily interested in South American passenger and freight services. For the freighters, the firm offered two sailings per week from New York. The mainline service sailed to Rio de Janeiro, Santos, Montevideo and Buenos Aires; the secondary run was to Belem, Fortaleza, Recife, Bahia and Rio de Janeiro.

Outward-bound for Brazil, the Victory-class freighter *Mormacpine* passes Lower Manhattan. (James McNamara Collection)

Anti-clockwise from *left*:

A big C3-class freighter, the 492ft-long *Mormacgulf*, passes Lower Manhattan. (James McNamara Collection)

Six Moore-McCormack Lines freighters at the company's 23rd Street terminal in Brooklyn. (Moore-McCormack Lines)

Heavy lift onto the *Mormactrade* at Brooklyn. (Moore-McCormack Lines)

Completed in 1961, the *Mormaclake* represented a new class of more modern and efficient cargo liners. (James McNamara Collection)

Argentine State Line

State-owned and based at Buenos Aires, this company ran services between the east coast of South America and US East Coast and Gulf ports.

Delta Line

When they were built just after World War Two ended in 1946, three brand-new combination passenger and cargo liners for New Orleans-based Delta Line were among the finest ships of their type. Joining the company's fleet of freighters and with considerable cargo space of their own, they could also carry 119 passengers in especially luxurious, high-quality, comfortable quarters. Named *Del Norte*, *Del Mar* and *Del Sud*, they were actually built on American standardised C-3-type freighter hulls, but then redesigned with, among other changes, an extended superstructure for both passengers and crew quarters.

The 10,000-ton *Del Norte*, the first of the trio, was launched at the Ingalls Shipbuilding Corporation yard at Pascagoula, Mississippi, in May 1946. Her two sisters were also notable; they were among the first commercial ships with an added navigational aid – radar. Their exteriors were also quite modern, highlighted by a flat 'dummy stack' that actually housed officers' quarters, while twin silver-painted uptakes were the actual exhausts. Outdoor amenities included a pool and umbrella-lined lido area.

Delta Line's *Del Aires* arriving at New Orleans. (Alex Duncan)

Internally, they boasted air conditioning and private bathrooms in every passenger cabin. They could also boast of the most modern crew quarters yet to put to sea – 125 staff housed in forty cabins, all of them air-conditioned. Passenger facilities also included a barber's shop, special ladies' lounge and, uniquely, eight wedge-shaped staterooms that were located in the curved, forward part of the superstructure. They were among the first passenger-carrying ships to eliminate upper berths and use only beds. They also featured an exceptional three-cabin 'suite' combination that, when measured, totalled 1,000 square feet.

The Delta Line was well established in the US–South America trade. In addition to the above-mentioned ships, Delta operated some fifteen freighters, many of which carried up to twelve passengers. While they invested in the passenger and general freight trades, the company's ships had large capacities to deliver Brazilian coffee to the States. In fact, so pressing was the demand for coffee that Delta Line ran commercial sailings out of South American ports well into World War Two, until as late as 1943.

Delta also played a special part in American social history. 'It is said that the Delta Line invented the 3 o'clock coffee break,' according to Captain James McNamara, who served with Delta Line in the late sixties. 'The Delta New Orleans offices in the 1920s used to have an afternoon coffee break. The idea soon spread around the country.'

The three 16½-knot sisters worked a regular forty-four-day round-trip service from New Orleans and Houston to St Thomas, Rio de Janeiro, Santos and Buenos Aires, then returning via Santos, Rio and Curaçao. In 1967, however, they were downgraded to twelve-passenger freighters.

Captain McNamara, later president of the National Cargo Bureau, was aboard the 493ft-long *Del Norte* in her twilight years. He recalled:

We had parked cars along the Promenade Deck in the late sixties. Once happy and busy ships, they were actually quite sad vessels in the end. The once impeccable public rooms were then dusty and the piano in the lounge was covered over. Just twenty years of age, they really had shortened lives.

In 1972, having completed their final all-cargo South America trip and against rising operational costs for American-flag vessels, they were retired. In a single transaction, the trio was sold to a Taiwanese scrap merchant and promptly sailed to Kaohsiung to be dismantled.

Booth Line

This British-flag firm was rather unique in shipping – they traded regularly to the remote Amazon, on 1,000-mile voyages to Manaus. There were two sailings per month from Liverpool, calling at Lisbon and Madeira, and then to Belem, Recife, Manaus and with some sailings as far as Iquitos. Booth also ran a Caribbean service, which included separate sailings from New York to St Kitts, Antigua, Guadeloupe, Dominica, Martinique, St Lucia, St Vincent and Grenada.

Named mostly for early saints, some Booth ships were quite small, such as the 1,500grt *Clement*, and consequently had accommodation for as few as four to six passengers.

Priscilla Corbett and I met aboard a North Atlantic crossing, in the lavish comforts of Cunard's mighty *Queen Mary 2*. She attended my talks, mostly about bygone passenger ships and one just devoted to British ships. These sparked family memories. She told me:

> My grandfather and then my father worked for the Booth Line, based at Liverpool. Booth and their ships were rather unique – from England they sailed to Brazil and in particular to the Amazon River. After leaving the famed River

Mersey, Booth ships called in at Portugal, Spain and Madeira before crossing over to Trinidad, Barbados and then doing the 1,000-mile voyage along the Amazon to Manaus. Often, smaller Booth ships would go even farther, passing Manaus and going to Iquitos.

The lure of sea and maybe a family seafaring tradition are often strong:

> My father followed his father to sea and even after he and his ship were torpedoed during World War Two, in 1942. His ship was a freighter. He later told me it was an unforgettable sight – 'So awful, full of death and destruction and heads bobbing in the dark waters. Dark brown smoke lingered from where his ship had sunk.'

Booth Line was known, until the early 1960s, for their passenger-cargo ships on that run to and from the Amazon. They carried up to 200 passengers (in two classes) and lots of freight. Priscilla continued:

> My father served in the fifties on the *Hildebrandt*, *Hilary* and *Hubert*, each a passenger ship. Their voyages were, he said, very warm, often thickly humid trips along the river. The round-trips, Liverpool and back to Liverpool, took two

Booth Line's 1,500-ton *Clement* was used in the New York–West Indies service. (Author's Collection)

months. At Manaus, the crew would trade with the locals, the Indians. In return for woodcarvings and even carved animal teeth, the Indians wanted buckets of the ship's paint. They then used the paint on their bodies, as decorations.

My father later served at New York, on the Booth Line's freighter service from there to the Caribbean and Brazil. They were very small freighters, but sometimes carrying as few as six passengers each.

Through a subsidiary known as the Booth-American Steamship Company, their ships – with names like *Clement* and *Crispin* – sailed, usually on Friday afternoons, from Pier 1 at the foot of Fulton Street in Brooklyn.

Booth vanished completely from the sea lanes by the early 1980s. Shipping had changed, but memories do indeed linger. Priscilla concluded, 'I still have my father's cap and a Booth Line teaspoon as memories of him and his life at sea and going up the Amazon.'

Lloyd Brasileiro

The author best remembers the freighters of Brazil's Lloyd Brasileiro for their rather distinctive funnels. Commissioned soon after World War Two in 1947, the 443ft-long *Loide-Bolivia* was one of twenty identical sisters built for this company.

Chilean Line

Also known as CSAV – Compañía Sudamericana de Vapores – this company ran a twice-monthly service to Valparaíso, Antofagasta, Arica, Callao, Cristóbal and US East Coast ports.

Grancolombiana

A consortium created by mixed South American interests, each specialising in the northbound coffee trades to the US, the handsome ships of Grancolombiana dominated the upper Brooklyn waterfront. The author well remembers often the sight of two of these ships berthed at the foot of Furman Street in Brooklyn Heights and just across from Lower Manhattan. Once having a large fleet, Grancolombiana was disbanded in the 1980s.

Blue Star Line

They were probably best remembered, according to the author, by their large (often very large) funnels. Indeed, they were distinctive and very handsome ships. The funnels often bore oversized stars, which complimented the 'Star' nomenclature used by the Blue Star Line.

London-based Blue Star is known for its South American service – from the UK and north European ports to Lisbon, Madeira, Tenerife, Rio de Janeiro, Santos, Montevideo and Buenos Aires. This was based on general freight going outwards to South America, with coffee and especially Argentine beef on the return. Blue Star was part of the Vestey Group, which also owned a large chain of butchers shops in the UK. Affiliate companies included the likes of the Booth Line and Lamport & Holt Line.

Blue Star also operated a monthly freighter service between the UK, Curaçao, the Panama Canal and the American West Coast: Los Angeles, San Francisco, Seattle, Portland, Victoria and Vancouver. There were two further services: UK–South and East Africa (Cape Town, Port Elizabeth, East London, Durban, Lourenço Marques and Beira) and from the UK and US ports via Panama to various Australian and New Zealand ports.

With a unique funnel device, the *Loide-Venezuela* was one of a series of freighters built for Lloyd Brasileiro. (Alex Duncan)

In 1957, when John Malone was 15, he was just old enough to run away to sea – as a galley boy aboard the once large Blue Star Line. He was off aboard one of that company's big freighters, the *Australia Star*, and his very first trip was a roaring introduction to life at sea – it was a trip around the world that took six months. Decades later, John recalled:

We sailed from London down to South America, to Rio de Janeiro and Buenos Aires, then over to South Africa, to Cape Town, Port Elizabeth and Durban. Then it was up to Lourenço Marques and Beira before heading across the Indian Ocean to New Zealand, to Wellington, Napier and Auckland. We loaded meat in those ports. Then it was up to the Panama Canal, Kingston, Trinidad, Barbados and finally home to London. It was quite an initiation – and I gained lots of experience. And it was an initiation to life itself. I earned £3 or about $15 a week. When the other very young lads in the crew went ashore, we'd buy one drink each and then sip it for hours. Going back to the ship, we never had money for a taxi.

The luxurious passenger lounge aboard Hamburg South America's twelve-passenger freighter, Cap Frio. (Author's Collection)

Hamburg South America Line

Trading in North America as the Columbus Line, this historic West German shipping line serviced ports along the East Coast of North America, both from northern Europe and North America. In 2017, Hamburg Sud, as it was widely known, then a large container ship operator, was acquired by Denmark's Maersk Line.

Hamburg South America Line's *Santa Isabel*, seen here at Hamburg, also carried twenty-eight passengers. (Author's Collection)

A double-bedded passenger cabin aboard the *Burg Sparrenberg*, also of Hamburg South America Line. (Author's Collection)

The *Cap Blanco* at Hamburg. (Arnold Kludas Collection)

Chargeurs Réunis/Sud-Atlantique

These French shipping lines co-ordinated their freight services from Le Havre, Anvers, Dunkirk and Bordeaux. Chargeurs Réunis also ran separate services to Africa and the Far East.

Spain's Naviera Aznar traded to the Canaries and West Africa, and also to South America. Offloading fruits, their *Monte Urbasa* is moored at the New Fresh Wharves in London. (Author's Collection)

Italian Line's *Amerigo Vespucci*, which carried up to 600 passengers as well as cargo, sailed between Italy and South America for a time. (ALF Collection)

Johnson Line's *Argentina* at Curaçao. (ALF Collection)

Johnson Line

Swedish-owned Johnson Line offered services from Gothenburg and other Swedish ports and often via Antwerp to the east coast of South America: to Recife, Salvador, Rio de Janeiro, Santos, Paranagua, Rio Grande, Montevideo and Buenos Aires. There was also a service via Curaçao and the Panama Canal to the North American West Coast and Hawaii.

Fruits, Nuts and Gold Bullion: Africa

Farrell Lines

The US-flagged Farrell Lines all but dominated the South and East African freighter trade from New York in the 1950s and 1960s. The primary run was to Cape Town, Port Elizabeth, East London, Durban, Lourenço Marques and Beira. A secondary service to West Africa was offered, calling at Monrovia, Abidjan, Takoradi, Accra, Lagos, Apapa, Matadi, Luanda, Lobito, Pointe Noire and Douala.

After her maiden arrival in September 1961, the 572ft-long *African Comet* made the 6,786-mile passage from New York to Cape Town in twelve days, sixteen hours and twenty-two minutes, at an average speed of 22.31 knots. She broke all existing records on the US–South African run. The *Comet* and her sisters also carried twelve passengers in luxuriously comfortable accommodations.

Robin Line

A division of Moore-McCormack Lines, Robin Line – with its sleek, grey and silver-painted freighters – offered twice-monthly voyages between New York, other US East Coast ports and Cape Town, Port Elizabeth, East London, Durban, Lourenço Marques, Beira, Dar es Salaam, Zanzibar, Tanga, Mombasa and Tamatave. Robin lost its separate identity when it was fully integrated into Moore-McCormack in the 1960s.

During a maritime strike in 1965, four Farrell freighters are idle and nested together at Brooklyn. (Gillespie-Faber Collection)

Farrell Lines' *African Moon* gets underway, heading off to South and East African ports. (James McNamara Collection)

The *African Dawn* arrives in New York on her maiden voyage in 1962. (James McNamara Collection)

Robin Line's *Robin Doncaster* is handled by two Moran tugs as she arrives at Brooklyn's Eire Basin. (James McNamara Collection)

Elder Dempster Lines

In the still huge and mighty British Merchant Navy of the 1950s and 1960s, Elder Dempster Lines was the leading national carrier to West Africa. Their ships served ports (from the UK as well as from New York, Montreal, the Mediterranean and even India) in West Africa: Bathurst, Freetown, Monrovia, Tema, Lagos and countless smaller, often backwater ports.

Gordon Cooper was a junior officer aboard the 5,900grt freighter *Dixcove*. A motorship capable of 14 knots, the 460ft-long ship was completed in 1959. Having been with Blue Funnel, an even larger British shipowner, he transferred over to Elder Dempster following its takeover by Blue Funnel in 1967:

Elder Dempster's 5,900-ton *Degema* berthed at Liverpool. (Alex Duncan)

> Elder Dempster itself and the *Dixcove* were not quite up to Blue Funnel's high standards. It was less formal, more relaxed, not as strict. The *Dixcove* carried deck cargo as well as freight in the holds, but no passengers. We carried manufactured goods and oil rig equipment going out to West Africa; we returned with cocoa, coffee, latex, plywood, logs, fish and some rubber. There were lots of stops and some of the smaller ports in West Africa were not really ports at all, but just anchorages. The *Dixcove* moored offshore and loaded from there.

Gordon Cooper added:

> The West African pilots along with their wives would come aboard and navigate the various remote tributaries that were fan-shaped from the River Niger. The ports had names like Wari and Sapele and Port Harcourt. Tucked away were the headquarters of various oil companies. Consequently, Elder Dempster also carried lots of oil piping. Some pipes were so large that they had to be loaded at Liverpool at an angle and then slanted downward into a hatch. In the UK, we had the advantage of dockside cranes, but in West Africa we had to use four of the ship's derricks. The piping had to be jostled out very, very carefully – and then finally levelled and lifted. It would take days of training to have the derrick operators and Africans work closely together.
>
> One of the early voyages on the *Dixcove* was a long one – from Liverpool to West African ports then across to the US East Coast, to Jacksonville, Savannah, Baltimore, Philadelphia and finally New York, but there was a dockers' strike. We were there, at a Brooklyn pier, for three weeks. But once loading began, there were more troubles: the dockers had difficulty loading some heavy machinery and even damaged one of the pieces.

Loading at Hamburg, the *King Jaja* of Nigerian National Lines. (Arnold Kludas Collection)

Ellerman Lines

This very large company and group had as many as seventy-five ships by the 1960s. These were divided into several subsidiaries: City Line, Hall Line, Ellerman & Papayanni Lines, Ellerman & Bucknall Steam Ship Co. and the Westcott & Laurence Line. Suffice it to say, their services were worldwide.

'I had the hottest curry of my entire life on an Ellerman Lines' ship,' remembered Alan Parkhurst. He worked for Ellerman in their claims department in Durban. He would check the freight, often well into the night and sometimes under the hottest conditions:

The captain's quarters aboard the *City of Brooklyn*, commissioned in 1949. (Ellerman Lines)

Getting away: *City of London* heads off for South African ports. (Ellerman Lines)

Outbound on the *City of Sydney*. (Ellerman Lines)

We had lots of freighters, most of which carried up to twelve passengers each. Our chairman, Sir John Ellerman, selected one, the *City of Johannesburg*, as his personal yacht. Expectedly, that ship had the very best care and maintenance, and the twelve passenger berths were used by Sir John and his friends and associates.

Living in the UK as well as southern Africa, Mr and Mrs Henry Dahl travelled on many passenger liners. But occasionally, they would sail in passenger-carrying freighters. 'Often, we enjoyed the very beautiful ships of the Ellerman Lines,' they remembered:

We especially recall the twelve-passenger *City of Hull*. We travelled in that ship from London to Durban – and it was sheer luxury! The ship had the most beautiful drawing room, the most splendid china, turbaned stewards and even an Indian hairdresser who came to your cabin.

The *City of Lucknow* arrives in Sydney. (Ellerman Lines)

Vast and filled with ships, part of the London Docks, 1952. (Port of London Authority)

Handling cargo: Canadian Pacific's *Maplecove* is on the right; Holland America's *Dalerdyk* on the left. (Port of London Authority)

British India Steam Navigation

In one book on merchant shipping, the author noted that the routes of British India, even in the 1960s, were too numerous to list. Quite simply, he wrote, British India has a network of services that covers the entire Indian Ocean, but with extended services that connect to the UK, the Far East and Australia/New Zealand. Formally titled the British India Steam Navigation Co. Ltd and with headquarters in London as well as management offices in Bombay and Calcutta, BI – as it was often called – was owned, in fact, by P&O. There is more about British India in Chapter 5.

South African Marine Corporation's *Constantia* outbound from Cape Town. (Gillespie-Faber Collection)

Holland-Africa Line

An arm of the United Netherlands Steamship Co., this firm traded between north European ports and South and East Africa (as well as to the Middle East and Australia).

Union-Castle Line

Noted for its large passenger-ship fleet, London-based Union-Castle Line also ran freighters to ports in Africa. They were noted for carrying large quantities of fruits northward from African ports to the UK.

Lloyd Triestino

This Italian firm offered services to Africa from Italy (as well as to the Middle East, Far East and Australia).

Compañía Colonial

Along with another Lisbon-based firm, Compañía Nacional, Compañía Colonial ran services to and from Portuguese West and East Africa.

Nouvelle Compagnie Havraise Péninsulaire de Navigation

This French-flagged company ran freighter services to East Africa, Indian Ocean islands and the Middle East.

Exotic waters: Brocklebank Line's *Mangla* is the centrepiece in this Stephen Card painting. (Stephen Card)

Gathering of ships: Royal Interocean Lines' *Straat Soenda* is berthed at Hong Kong with the passenger liners *Marco Polo* and *President Cleveland* behind. (Des Kirkpatrick Collection)

Belonging to Iran's Arya Shipping Lines, the *Arya Shahob* is berthed at Brooklyn. (Author's Collection)

Bibby Line's passenger-cargo liner *Leicestershire*, on the UK–Burma run, is seen entering the Gladstone Dock, Liverpool, with *Reina Del Pacifico* on the left. (Kenneth Wrightman, Mick Lindsay Collection)

Bound for Rangoon: another Bibby Line ship, the *Staffordshire*, loading in London Docks. (Kenneth Wrightman, Mick Lindsay Collection)

Beautiful design: among the best-looking freighters of the post-war era was *Port Auckland*, commissioned in 1949 and weighing 11,945 tons and 560ft in length. (Mick Lindsay Collection)

Australian service: New Zealand Shipping Co.'s *Piako*, but now in P&O colours and berthed at Sydney. (Mick Lindsay Collection)

Busy day: the *Canton* of P&O is in centre position in this view of the London Docks. A Glen Line freighter is on the left; a ship from Shaw Savill on the right. (Mick Lindsay Collection)

Celebration: the 15,896grt eighty-five-passenger *Ceramic* dressed in flags for an unspecified occasion in the Royal Docks, London. (Kenneth Wrightman, Mick Lindsay Collection)

Shaw Savill's *Cretic* being handled by tugs in the Thames. (Kenneth Wrightman, Mick Lindsay Collection)

Careful handling: another Shaw Savill freighter, the *Doric*, is being moved from the Gladstone Dock to the Hornby Dock at Liverpool. (Kenneth Wrightman, Mick Lindsay Collection)

Shaw Savill's *Gothic* looking immaculate as she steams past Gravesend. (Kenneth Wrightman, Mick Lindsay Collection)

Bow out: Shaw Savill's 13,587-ton *Suevic* at Wellington. (Mick Lindsay Collection)

New Zealand waters: dating from 1960, the *Icenic* at Wellington. (Mick Lindsay Collection)

Right: In port: Shaw Savill's *Megantic* and the Matson liner *Monterey* at Suva, Fiji, in 1970. (Mick Lindsay Collection)

Right: Another New Zealand Co. ship, the *Otaio*, is seen here later in her career wearing P&O colours. (Dave Vincent, Mick Lindsay Collection)

Left: Dominated by her tall, pale yellow funnel, the 488ft-long *Piako* of New Zealand Shipping Co. (Mick Lindsay Collection)

Great gathering of ships: *Rangitiki* is one of five ships seen in this evocative view of the Royal Albert Dock. (Mick Lindsay Collection)

Opposite: Shaw Savill's *Wairangi* rests in the Langton Dock, Liverpool. (Kenneth Wrightman, Mick Lindsay Collection)

The *Otaio*, the New Zealand Shipping Co.'s training ship, turning in the Royal Docks on 8 April 1963. (Kenneth Wrightman, Mick Lindsay Collection)

The *Kaimiro*, of the Union Steamship Co. of New Zealand. The 345-footer was built in 1956. (Mick Lindsay Collection)

Blue Funnel's *Peleus*, which could also carry up to thirty passengers, is seen berthed at Hong Kong. (Mick Lindsay Collection)

Having classic Blue Funnel design, the 1947-built *Calchas* is seen with a yellow funnel while under charter. presumably to Elder Dempster Lines. (Mick Lindsay Collection)

Completed in 1963, the *Centaur* of Blue Funnel was purposely designed for the western Australia–Singapore trade, carrying sheep, general cargo and up to 190 passengers. (Mick Lindsay Collection)

The mighty looking *Phrontis* had been built in 1967 as Glen Line's *Pembrokeshire* but transferred to Blue Funnel in 1972. (Mick Lindsay Collection)

Glen Line's *Glenbeg*, seen outbound in the Thames, was the *Samjack*, a 1944-built Liberty ship. Bought by Blue Funnel in 1947 and renamed *Tydeus*, she was moved over to the Glen Line in 1950. (Mick Lindsay Collection)

The imposing *Glenfruin*, also of Glen Line, approaching the Royal Docks, London. (Kenneth Wrightman, Mick Lindsay Collection)

Glen Line's *Flintshire* was built in Holland in 1962. She transferred to Blue Funnel as shown here in 1974 and then later finished her days for Singapore owners as the *Orient Express*. (Mick Lindsay Collection)

Another big Glen Line freighter, the *Glenroy*, waits in the London Docks. At 8,959 tons and built in 1938, she served during World War Two as a fleet supply ship. Topped by a large funnel, the 507ft-long *Glenroy* also had quarters for up to eighteen passengers. (Kenneth Wrightman, Mick Lindsay Collection)

Well known on the UK–Australia run, Federal Steam Navigation Co. had a large fleet of freighters named after British counties. In this view, the *Middlesex* is about to berth in the King George V Dock in April 1959. (Kenneth Wrightman, Mick Lindsay Collection)

Ben Line was an important carrier between the UK and ports in the Middle and Far East. Built in 1946, the *Benarkle* had been Ellerman Lines' *City of Poona*, having been purchased by Ben in 1968. She was scrapped in 1974. (Mick Lindsay Collection)

American President Lines' *President Monroe*, seen here at Boston, and her sister were used in continuous three-month round-the-world service. (ALF Collection)

Advertising: Matson's classic C2-class freighter *Hawaiian Pilot* was recreated as a put-together plastic model. The box cover featured this painting. (Author's Collection)

One of American Pioneer Lines' big, fast Mariner-class, the 21-knot *Pioneer Main* berthed at Philadelphia. (Norman Knebel Collection)

Hamburg America and North German Lloyd often offered joint services. Here is the 1965-built *Alemannia*, used on the north Europe–Pacific service and already carrying a good number of containers. (Mick Lindsay Collection)

Hamburg America used many of its smaller freighters on their varied services such as the 4,000-ton *Duisberg*, seen here in Holland's New Waterway. (Kenneth Wrightman, Mick Lindsay Collection)

A classic combination passenger-cargo liner, the *Hannover* was one of six sisters that plied the Europe–Far East route. Hamburg America had three, North German Lloyd the other three. The *Hannover* also carried eighty-six passengers in luxurious quarters. She is seen here in July 1966. (Kenneth Wrightman, Mick Lindsay Collection)

Night time in Brooklyn: Orient Overseas Lines' *Pacific Reliance* and *Hong Kong Exporter* in May 1970. (Author's Collection)

5

Smelling of Teas and Spices: India and the Middle East

Nedlloyd

The freighter operations of two of Holland's biggest and best-known shipping lines, Nederland Line and Royal Rotterdam Lloyd, were merged as Nedlloyd. 'Nedlloyd had some especially sturdy ships that often included heavy-lift booms and equipment and often had superb accommodations for passengers as well,' noted Captain James McNamara:

> They sailed between US East and Gulf ports and the Middle East as well as to Indonesia. Outwards, their ships carried general cargo including chemicals and heavy lifts; on the return trips, they were loaded with the likes of jute, burlap and carpet backing.

A New York agent for Nedlloyd in the 1960s recalled:

> These ships were very popular with older, often retired passengers, who wanted an often long, very unique, affordable voyage to Mid-Eastern ports or completely around the world. A four-month round voyage to the Middle East from New York and return was priced from $1,400.

As an example, the twelve-passenger freighter *Raki* departed from New York (from Brooklyn's Bush Terminal) on 1 December 1963 for Tripoli, Alexandria, Lattakia, Beirut, Port Said,

A trio of Royal Rotterdam Lloyd freighters along with the liner *Willem Ruys* at Rotterdam. (Nico Guns Collection)

Royal Rotterdam Lloyd's *Ampenam* loading at Rotterdam on 19 January 1951. (Nico Guns Collection)

The heavy-lift crane *Hercules* loads a small boat aboard Royal Rotterdam Lloyd's *Bantam* at Rotterdam on 7 April 1950. (Nico Guns Collection)

Aqaba, Karachi, Bombay, Cochin, Trincomalee, Chittagong, Calcutta, China, Penang, Port Swettenham, Singapore, Hong Kong, Yokohama, Nagoya, Kobe, Valparaíso, Arica, Matarani, Callao, Guayaquil, Buenaventura, Manta, Cristóbal, Houston, New Orleans and finally back to New York.

Isthmian Lines

Until the 1960s, US-flagged Isthmian Lines offered five distinct freighter services from their large terminal in New York Harbor, at Brooklyn's Erie Basin. There was an India–Pakistan–Ceylon service; Mediterranean–Red Sea run; Persian Gulf service; a round-the-world service with emphasis on South East Asia; and, in a joint operation with the Matson Line, a run to Hawaii via the Panama Canal.

Captain McNamara said:

Isthmian was a division, until 1955, of United States Steel and then afterward owned by States Marine Lines. There were twenty-four C-3 class freighters used in service between the US East Coast, the Middle East, the Persian Gulf, Indonesia and Hawaii. Isthmian pulled out of the freighter trades in 1973, however.

British India Line

Helen Routledge was married, in the late sixties, to a chief engineer on the now long-vanished British India Line, a classic, long-established shipping company that was straight out of the pages of the British Empire. More formally, even its name hinted at a bygone age: the British India Steam Navigation Company Limited:

My husband never served on the BI passenger ships, but on freighters only – the *Bombala*, *Bulimba*, *Merkara* and *Jelunga*. It was an interesting life, but very different life. Sometimes, we would sit at anchor in places like Karachi and Calcutta for weeks, even as long as a month. We'd just wait. At times, the days and nights seemed endless. Fortunately, I had my Singer sewing machine – and sewed and sewed and sewed! I also ran the ship's bar at night. Once a week, we had those one-reel films. They were sent out by the seamen's missions. Some of them were pretty awful films, but watching them helped pass the time. But sometimes, we lost power – and for several days. Then we had to hand flush

The *Steel Scientist* arriving at Philadelphia. (James McNamara Collection)

the toilets. Of course, we had lots of curries for our meals. And I remember we'd sometimes have young cadets on-board. They were teenagers, never been to sea in their lives and they would be so seasick. They wouldn't just be pale, but sheet white!

A link to the old Empire – Martin Shawcross served briefly, back in the 1950s, with British India. 'My first BI ship was the freighter *Chantala*, which was also the company's training ship,' he told me:

She carried up to forty cadets plus forty-four regular crew and twelve passengers. Altogether there was close to 100 on-board. You'd never have that, say, these days and where huge containerships often have less than two dozen crew members. The *Chantala* was on BI's UK–Australia service. Later, I went to BI's O-class freighters, which sailed between Bombay and Karachi and then to Malaysia, Hong Kong and Japan. In some areas, in the fifties, we were still on alert for mines left over from World War Two. We carried all sorts of cargo – such as dates and cotton and even scrap metal from India to the Far East, and then returned with items such as sulfur, carbon, sugar and even newspaper.

'If you were blind and travelled the different British ships of, say, the 1960s, there is one way you could differentiate between the various shipping lines themselves,' noted ship's engineer, Barrie Beavis:

On Cunarders on the New York run, it was mostly the smell of American cigarettes. On Union-Castle, it was the smells of African fruits and spices. On P&O and British India, it was the smell of Indian curries, and on the Royal Mail Lines, it was rum, coffee and raw sugar.

British India – with its charismatically named passenger and cargo ships – began in 1856 as the evocatively named Calcutta & Burmah Steam Navigation Co. Ltd. Owned by P&O from 1914, by 1972 it was finally more fully integrated into that London-based company's operation. By then, British India owned some 500 ships and managed another 150.

By the 1980s, the British India Steam Navigation Company Limited had vanished completely from those eastern sea lanes. The passenger ship *Dwarka* was their last commercial ship, then operating out of Bombay to a collection of Persian Gulf ports. The 4,800-tonner was decommissioned

The 6,700grt *Barpeta* of the British India Steam Navigation Co. Ltd. Completed in 1960, she and her sisters used the engines-aft design. (ALF Collection)

in April 1982. But the *Uganda*, a former passenger-cargo ship used on the London–East Africa route and later an educational-style cruise ship, was the last BI ship in operation. Used during the Falklands War and continuing with a British Government charter, she was withdrawn in 1985.

Bank Line

This well-known British shipping line (managed by Andrew Weir & Co. Ltd) had, by the early 1960s, almost fifty freighters trading on no fewer than eight routes: India–South Africa, Far East–South Africa, US Gulf–Australia and New Zealand, US–Far East, India–east coast of South America, UK–South Pacific islands and US East Coast–Middle East.

Brocklebank Line

This British line, primarily serving between UK ports and the Middle East, was noted for its 'M' nomenclature – with ships such as the *Magdapur*, *Mahanada* and *Mahout*.

Clan Line

Also British, this company was noted for its 'Clan' naming – with ships such as the *Clan Farquharson* and *Clan Macinnes*. It traded between the UK, the Middle East and Australia and also between Africa and Australia.

Hoegh Lines

Norwegian shipowner Leif Hoegh operated as the Hoegh Line and, among others, offered monthly sailings from the US East Coast to the Middle East, Karachi, Bombay, Cochin, Colombo, Madras and Calcutta. Up to twelve passengers were carried on-board large freighters such as the *Hoegh Dyke*. West German-built, this 17-knot ship was well suited to Mid-Eastern service – she was especially designed to carry vegetable oils, liquid latex, lube oils and other liquids.

Royal Interocean Lines

Renamed from the Dutch colonial Java-China Packet Line after World War Two, Royal Interocean Lines was Dutch-owned but never visited Holland. With a large fleet including half a dozen passenger ships, it traded on almost a dozen world routes. Touching on three continents and creating a four-month round-trip, the longest included the Middle East and was routed from Buenos Aires, Santos, Montevideo and Rio de Janeiro to Cape Town, Port Elizabeth, East London, Durban, Mauritius, Penang, Port Swettenham, Singapore, Manila, Hong Kong, Kobe and finally a turnaround at Yokohama.

On some remote services, many Royal Interocean freighters carried passengers. Occasionally during their travels, Mr and Mrs Henry Dahl travelled by freighter. 'We had a delightful trip on a little vessel, the Dutch *Tjipanjet* of the Royal Interocean Lines,' they recalled:

> She carried only three passengers. There was one double and one single. An Indonesian steward looked after the officers and the passengers. You could never buy a drink, however. The ship's jovial Dutch captain always insisted. Consequently, it was often said that he spent more money on his three passengers than the combined captains of the far larger Royal Interocean passenger liners, *Ruys*, *Boissevain* and *Tegelberg*, which each carried several hundred passengers.

Hansa Line

West Germany's Hansa Line was perhaps best known for its heavy-lift ships, handling large industrial cargos. Its freighters often had a useful engines-aft design, practical for large deck cargos, as well as heavy-lift cranes.

Hansa traded to the Middle East – from New York via Suez to Djeddah, Port Soudan, Djibouti, Aden, ports in the Persian Gulf, Karachi, Bombay, Colombo, Madras, Calcutta and Rangoon.

Captain James McNamara said:

> Hansa Line freighters often carried railway cars, especially old steam engines that were retired in the 1950s and 1960s by American railroads and that were sold for further service in the Middle East. These freighters also carried oil

Ships such as Bank Line's *Beaverbank* sailed out to Middle Eastern destinations from British and North European ports. (Arnold Kludas Collection)

company cargos including big cooling towers. They also carried a few of the early containers, some of which were placed forward in the bow section.

Concordia Line

Serving the Mediterranean and Middle East, this company was an arm of Norwegian shipowner, Christian Haaland.

Meats and Wool: Australia and New Zealand

P&O

In addition to their large and well-known fleet of passenger liners, P&O – the Peninsular & Oriental Steam Navigation Co. – operated freighters, some of which carried up to twelve passengers in service from the UK to the Middle and Far East, and to Australia and New Zealand.

In the early 1950s, Philip Jackson joined his first ship, P&O's 7,700grt *Socotra*. He recalled:

We sailed from the Royal Docks in London and then called at several north European ports: Bremen, Antwerp and Rotterdam on the first of several four-month long round-trips. Outwards, we carried mostly general cargo: manufactured goods, motor cars, steel and cement. Homeward, we had sheepskins, wool, timber and tinned fruit.

Port Line

'Some Port Line ships were the most handsome on all the seas,' noted former crewmember, Geoff Palmer:

They were sleek and well balanced. But some also had noticeably extended superstructures, almost appearing to be passenger–cargo ships carrying, say, a hundred or so passengers. And although they had light grey hulls, they did not have Cunard funnel colours and so were sometimes confused to be Cunard ships.

Owned by Cunard, the Port Line operated as many as two dozen freighters (in 1960) and traded between UK ports and Australia/New Zealand and also, as a member of the American & Australian Line, sailed from the likes of Montreal, New York and other US East Coast ports. Port Line ceased services in 1978.

American & Australian Line

A consortium of British freighter companies offered services from New York and other US East Coast ports to Australia and New Zealand. One of New York's biggest and busiest shipping agencies, Norton Lilly & Company, represented a consortium of British shipowners that ran a service from US ports to Australia and New Zealand. These included the Federal Line, Port Line, New Zealand Shipping Company and the Ellerman Lines, which had a vast fleet of 'city ships'.

Shaw Savill Line

More formally Shaw Savill & Albion Co. Ltd, this long-established, well-known British shipping line had freighter interests between the UK and Australia or New Zealand. These included four big, combination passenger-cargo sister ships: *Athenic*, *Ceramic*, *Corinthic* and *Gothic*.

New Zealand Shipping Co.

Owned by P&O and using British registry, this company had quite large freighters as well as passenger-cargo liners on the UK and US runs to New Zealand.

7

Silks, Autos and Mass Produce: The Far East and the Pacific

Blue Funnel Line

Once one of the mightiest and best-known shipping firms, the Blue Funnel Line had a vast fleet that was dubbed, because of its ships' distinctive blue-coloured funnels, the 'Blue Flues'. Using Greek mythological names and having a fleet numbering more than sixty ships in the early sixties, the fleet was also dubbed 'the Birkenhead Navy'.

Blue Funnel ships sailed from Birkenhead, just across the Mersey from Liverpool, while affiliate Glen Line and Shire Line, also British flag, were based at London. Blue Funnel, part of Alfred Holt & Co., also included Ocean Steam Ship Co. Ltd and China Mutual Steam Navigation Co. Ltd. There was also a Dutch-flag affiliate of Blue Funnel.

The fleet was headed by eight sister and near-sister ships – the Jason and Pyrrhus classes – which also carried up to thirty passengers. They, along with other company ships, offered three sailings per month, from the UK to Port Said, Aden, Colombo, Penang, Port Swettenham, Singapore, Hong Kong, Kobe and Yokohama. Four others, the *Pyrrhus* and her sisters *Peleus*, *Patroclus* and *Perseus*, which also had quarters for up to thirty passengers, sailed to Australia – to Port Said, Aden, Fremantle, Adelaide, Melbourne and Sydney.

Gordon Cooper joined Blue Funnel in 1967 and was soon assigned to the 8,530grt freighter *Machaon* as a deck cadet:

Blue Funnel was still a great company – and a large company with over fifty ships. I had to keep a detailed Midship Log of details of my voyages and which was looked over by a senior officer. It was like keeping a journal at school. I joined the *Machaon* at Birkenhead, just across from Liverpool. She'd come down from Glasgow and then we crossed to Dublin, where we loaded huge drums, like tanks, of Guinness. There was also lots of Scotch Whisky loaded at Glasgow. We had to be especially careful of the dockers at Dublin. The Scotch and the Guinness were tempting. We also had steel coils and lots of manufactured goods aboard and then sailed out via Suez to the Far East.

Blue Funnel's *Peleus* discharging in Hong Kong. (James L. Shaw Collection)

Four Blue Funnel freighters line the docks at Birkenhead (with the River Mersey and Liverpool behind) in 1966. Three Clan Line freighters are just behind. (Blue Funnel Line)

Glen Line's *Denbighshire* moored at Genoa on 2 June 1963. A Mitsui-OSK Line freighter is on the left. (Michael Cassar Collection)

The usual trip out to the Far East and back was three months, but expanded to four when the Suez closed and ships had go via the South African Cape. Just before Suez closed in June 1967, we were warned not to go through. We might be trapped. We waited with a Ben Line freighter, then an affiliate to Blue Funnel. But the Blue Funnel captain decided to go through. The Ben ship reversed course, passed back through the Med and used the Cape route. We were lucky – we made it! Our ship picked up all the cargo in the Far East whereas the Ben ship was a month late and lost out. But two northbound Blue Funnel ships, the *Melampus* and *Agapenor*, were stopped and trapped. They later had to be written-off and signed over to insurance underwriters.

Ships such as the 495ft-long *Machaon* were classic freighters, in a way, the last of a long line of ships:

The booms were called derricks and where always stowed on Blue Funnel ships. And, of course, there was a big funnel painted in that classic blue with a black top. By the second half of the 1960s, container ships would be, and would look, much different.

Gordon Cooper later served on the Blue Funnel's *Ajax* and *Clytoneus*:

The return trips from the Far East to the UK had very varied cargos. From Japan, we'd carry canned Mandarin oranges and light manufactured goods: radios, televisions and washing machines. From Hong Kong, it was clothing. From Singapore, it was tanks of palm oil and latex as well as raw rubber in bales. From Malaysia, it was bagged coconuts and boxed plywood. And from Ceylon is more coconuts and boxed tea. The liquid palm oil and latex as well as the boxed plywood paid for the whole voyage. These were the big revenue makers.

He added:

I was making $8,000–9,000 a year at Blue Funnel in 1967. Altogether, we had 35–40 crew aboard, five cargo holds, but the original 12 berths for passengers were by now only used by guests of the company. There was no air conditioning on-board except in the dining room and the bar. So, in the crew quarters, it was often sweltering. There were actually few crew comforts. The demand on the generators to operate electric fans when the ships were hot, humid ports was often problematic. There was, of course, decent food and cheap drinks at the bar. It was often said: 'You can find a British ship by the trail of empty beer cans!'

'It is indeed very sad that these great shipping lines, like Blue Funnel, are now gone completely,' concluded Cooper:

The once huge British Merchant Navy was all but gone by the 1980s. In the UK, the dockers and dock strikes were perhaps the most decisive blow. The costs became prohibitive. And so shipowners and their cargos went to European ports. And, of course, the transition and then expansion into containers was another blow. Many companies were not suited to this huge change. And finally, many of Britain's shipping management were unable to adjust. Shipping lines would lose experienced middle management, but keep on CEOs who were unwilling to compromise and adjust. Some were operating in the '70s and '80s as if it was still the '50s and '60s. These days [2017], Maersk Line is the largest container firm because, I feel, they have highly disciplined management.

More than most, Blue Funnel was considered one of the finest and best-run shipping companies not only in Britain but in the world. 'In shipping, they set the standards, very high standards,' recalled Robert Welding, a Liverpool seafarer in the 1950s and 1960s. 'Even their main offices, India House in Liverpool, were famous.'

Alfred Holt began thinking of shipping as far back as 1837, in the garden of his father's Liverpool home. It was said he thought of shipping, especially to the then very distant exotic Far East, as being like the Odyssey. And so, he gave his future ships Homeric names. Hundreds of Blue Funnel ships followed.

By the 1950s, Blue Funnel had one of the largest freighter fleets anywhere. But typically, change and then great change were ahead. The company faced the future and obtained its first container ship in 1969 and then added its last conventional freighters, the Maron class, in 1980. Ironically, these ships were built by Scotts Shipbuilding & Engineering Co. at Greenock, which in fact created the company's first new builds back in 1865.

But by the eighties the company struggled, finally lost interest in shipping and sold its very last ship, the LNG tanker *Nestor*, in 1989. Almost overnight, the once mighty Blue Funnel was no more.

A LIST OF OTHER FREIGHTER COMPANIES THAT WITHDREW FROM BRITISH SERVICE AFTER 1970

Henderson Line	1970
Port Line	1978
Furness Withy	1980
Wilson Line	1981
Union-Castle	1983
Pacific Steam – PSNC	1984
Anchor Line	1986
Booth Line	1986
British India	1986
Shaw Savill	1987
Blue Funnel	1989
Elder Dempster	1989
Fyffes Line	1990
Glen Line	1990
Ellerman Lines	1991
Ben Line	1991
Blue Star Line	2000
Harrison Line	2000

A big Federal Steam Navigation freighter is at the centre top of this view at Auckland in 1957. A Houlder Line freighter is to the right. Two liners, the *Monowai* and *Orcades*, are at the bottom. (ALF Collection)

Ben Line

Operating in partnership to provide a UK–Far Eastern ports service with Blue Funnel, Ben Line was another noted British shipowner. With a long history, they dated as far back as 1825, and were once noted for some very handsome-looking freighters. By the early 1960s, the company's largest ship was the 11,362grt *Benarmin*. She measured 550ft in length and, a motor ship with single screw, she could make up to 20 knots.

After dabbling in container ships, Ben Line withdrew from shipping in 1991 and afterward concentrated on port services and ship agency work. They remain in business to this day.

American President Lines

I well remember when the C3-class freighter *President Harding* came to the Bethlehem Steel shipyard, quite close to my home in Hoboken. Nearly 20 years of age and nearing her end of service under US subsidy operating laws, the 492ft-long ship had rather serious damage. There was an explosion in her forward hold, which blew large holes along both of the upper sides of the ship. She needed extensive and expensive repairs.

San Francisco-headquartered American President Lines was well known in New York Harbor, mostly from their busy terminal at Pier 9 in nearby Jersey City. That pier, located along the west side of the lower Hudson River, was very busy. Often two President ships were in port and at berth together – and as one departed, it seemed, another arrived.

Well known for their round-the-world service (voyages taking approximately 100 days), American President was strongly involved in US West Coast–Far East services, from San Francisco and Los Angeles to Honolulu, Yokohama, Kobe, Inchon, Pusan, Manila and Hong Kong.

In the 1970s, *Freighter Travel News*, a quarterly aimed at travellers preferring the intimacy, quiet atmosphere and informality of freighters, reported that American

Two new Mariner-class freighters, the *Palmetto Mariner* and the renamed *President Coolidge*, are being refitted and upgraded in Bethlehem Steel's Key Highway shipyard at Baltimore. (James McNamara Collection)

Three American President Lines freighters are seen in this 1959 view at San Francisco. A US Navy hospital ship and the liner *President Hoover* are also at berth. At bottom right is the laid-up liner *Leilani*. (American President Lines)

American President Lines ships at San Francisco during a 1962 maritime strike. Seven company ships were idle: *President Hoover* and *President Wilson* on the left; *President Taft* and *President Monroe* on the outer end; and on the right, *President Cleveland* with, nested together, the freighters *President Buchanan* and *President Grant*. (Author's Collection)

President Line's passenger-carrying ships were among the most comfortable, even most luxurious, on all the seas. This began especially in the mid-1950s with remodelled Mariner-class freighters such as the 560ft-long *President Jackson*.

Immediately popular, the 9,200-ton, 20-knot *Jackson* and her sisters would be booked by passengers months in advance. These ships handled the round-the-world service, calling at some two dozen ports. Quite successful, this class was followed by improved versions, the so-called Master Mariners, and others. However, many were later converted to partial and then full containerships.

American President Line was headed by several fine passenger liners, ships such as the sister ships *President Cleveland* and *President Wilson*, *President Hoover* and, largest and most luxurious of all, *President Roosevelt*. There were also two ninety-six-passenger combination passenger-cargo ships, *President Monroe* and *President Polk*. But while American President pulled out of liner services by 1972, it continued to carry up to a dozen passengers on many of its freighters until the early 1980s.

With rising operational costs under the US flag, as well as increased competition in shipping itself, American President was itself sold off (for $285 million) to Singapore-based Neptune Orient Line in 1998. Although American registry was gradually dropped altogether, American President – with large containerships – continues to this day, with American President Line names but flying flags of convenience. Neptune Orient, along with American President, was sold to Marseilles-based CMA-CGM, a huge container operator, in 2016.

Matson Line

Long established in the US West Coast–Hawaii trade, this San Francisco-based line remains in the container ship trade to this day.

Pacific Far East Line

One of the many US-flagged shipping lines operating from the American West Coast, they offered services to Yokohama, Kobe, Manila, Hong Kong and other Pacific ports.

States Lines

Another of the US West Coast shipping lines, States Lines serviced the Far East. But it suffered like many US-flag lines, with increasingly costly labour and an inability to compete with foreign-flag carriers. These companies disappeared from the sea lanes beginning in the 1970s.

Isbrandtsen

Isbrandtsen Line ran a sizeable fleet of freighters, all carrying break-bulk cargo and four to twelve passengers on three- and four-month round-the-world voyages. Their Victory-class ships had two four-bunk rooms and these were offered only to male travellers. After leaving their Brooklyn berths, they sailed to the Caribbean, passed through the Panama Canal and then crossed the Pacific to the Far East and South East Asia. Finally, they returned home via the Suez and the Mediterranean. Isbrandtsen *Flying Enterprise* made worldwide headlines when she foundered in January 1952, after a long heroic rescue effort during which her master remained on-board until the very final moments.

Dating from 1917, Isbrandtsen bought American Export Lines in 1960 and renamed it, by 1963, as American Export-Isbrandtsen Lines. Further acquisitions followed. However, with American Export-Isbrandtsen in deep financial troubles and then bankrupt by 1977, the company and its ships were sold to Farrell Lines.

In 2000, Farrell itself was sold to the big P&O-Nedlloyd group. Then, in 2006, P&O-Nedlloyd was acquired by Maersk Line. The last remnants of American Export-Isbrandtsen were in port operations, but were sold to Dubai Ports World in 2006 and the name disappeared.

American Pioneer Line

An arm of United States Lines, which looked after transatlantic services, American Pioneer traded from the West to the Far East and Australia. Along with several C2-class freighters, the company operated eight Mariner-class freighters. At 9,200 tons, with six hatches and capable of 20 knots, they were among the biggest freighters in the world in the late 1950s. These ships used an 'M' nomenclature – *Pioneer Ming*, *Pioneer Mill*, *Pioneer Moor*.

The author remembers that these big Mariners used Pier 4 on Staten Island on the inbound and offload. Then, usually on Thursday afternoons, they

Isbrandtsen's *Flying Enterprise II* is outbound from Baltimore. (Author's Collection)

The heavy-lift crane *Constellation* attends to the *Pioneer Ming* at Pier 61, New York. (United States Lines)

NYK Line's *Sanuki Maru* berthed at Vancouver. (ALF Collection)

Japan–South America service: the 8,516-ton *Santos Maru* was built by Mitsubishi Shipyards at Kobe in 1951. Originally designed as a twelve-passenger freighter, she was later converted to carry twelve in cabin class, fifty in special third class and 558 migrants in third class. (Hisashi Noma Collection)

would be shifted to Pier 61 in Manhattan. From that berth, they would load their outward cargos and, in several days, sail off to Panama and Far Eastern ports.

American Pioneer offered sailings every ten days in the late 1950s on the long-haul run to the Far East. The large, fast Mariner-class freighters, carrying twelve passengers, were routed from New York City to the Panama Canal, Honolulu, Manila, Hong Kong, Keelung, Kobe or Yokohama and Pusan. Passage fares in 1957 for the three weeks from New York to Hong Kong were posted at $400.

NYK (Nippon Yusen Kaisha) Line

Dating from 1870, NYK rose out of the ashes of World War Two, rebuilt its fleet and, by 2017, had over 900 ships of varied types. They were listed as one of the largest shipowners in the world. By the early 1950s, NYK had been able to revive many of its overseas freighter services. Even the 1930-built passenger ship *Hikawa Maru* was used in freighter service, carrying twelve passengers instead of 500. Soon, bigger, faster and more purposeful ships were created and were part of the great boom in Far Eastern cargo services in the 1950s and 1960s. (Other important Japanese shipowners in the fifties and sixties included the Mitsui Line, OSK Line, Shinnihon Line and the Kawasaki Line.)

In October 2016, Kawasaki Kisen Kaisha (the K Line), Mitsui OSK Lines and Nippon Yusen Kabushiki Kaisha (the NYK Line) agreed to merge their container shipping business by establishing a completely new, more competitive and efficient joint-venture company. The integration will also include their overseas terminal activities. The new company, renamed Ocean Network Express, will start operations from April 2018 and will have its holding company office in Tokyo, global headquarters in Singapore and regional headquarters in the United Kingdom (London), the United States (Richmond, VA), Hong Kong and Brazil (Sao Paulo).

Hamburg America Line/North German Lloyd

These famed, very historic shipowners (more fully merged in 1970 to become container giant Hapag-Lloyd) ran worldwide services on West German-flagged vessels. One of the most important was their Far East service, which was routed, using freighters, via Hamburg, Bremerhaven, Antwerp and Rotterdam to Port Said, Djibouti, Penang, Port Swettenham, Singapore, Miri, Manila, Hong Kong, Kobe and Yokohama. These ships were supported, beginning in 1953–54, by six notably luxurious 'combo' ships, carrying eighty-six first-class passengers each: *Frankfurt*, *Hamburg*, *Hannover*, *Bayernstein*, *Hessenstein* and *Schwabenstein*.

East Asiatic Company

This Copenhagen-based firm ran a port-intensive service out to South East Asia (as well as a service via Panama from northern Europe to the North American West Coast). The Asian itinerary was often routed from Copenhagen to Aarhus, Gothenburg, Oslo, Middlesbrough, Antwerp, Bremen, Hamburg, Rotterdam, London, Marseilles, Genoa, Port Said, Aden, Penang, Port Swettenham, Singapore, Bangkok and Saigon.

Later known as EAC, the company left the freighter trades in 1978 and closed down its remaining interests in 2014.

East Asiatic Company's *Manchuria*, used on the Europe-Far East run, is seen docked at the New Fresh Wharves at London. (Author's Collection)

Klaveness Line

Norway's A.F. Klaveness & Company sailed as the Klaveness Line – with ships such as the *Bronxville*, *Bonneville*, *Bougainville*, *Hopeville* and *Sunnyville* – and, until the 1960s, operated a long-haul service to the Far East and South East Asia.

Barber Lines

Barber Lines was the American operating name for a group of Norwegian freighter companies. Up until the 1970s, they were very active in their primary service to the Far East, offering weekly sailings from New York, Newport News, Charleston, through the Panama Canal, then from Los Angeles and San Francisco to Manila, Hong Kong, Bangkok, Singapore, Djakarta and then Kobe and Yokohama. This was marketed under the banner of Barber Lines.

The lines were Barber Wilhelmsen, also in Far East service, but with varied ports, and Barber Fern-Ville Lines, which offered services from Singapore, Port Swettenham, Penang, Belawan, Ceylon and Port Said to the US East Coast, including New York. There was also Barber West African Line, which offered twice-monthly sailings between New York and other US East Coast ports to Dakar, Monrovia, Takoradi, Lagos and Port Harcourt. Finally, the Oslo-based Wilhelmsen Line, on the North Atlantic, ran services between US East and Gulf Coast ports to Scandinavian ports.

Barber had shifted to container ships by the late 1970s.

Messageries Maritimes

This historic French company's services all but spanned the southern hemisphere, with special links to French and former French colonial outposts. With over three dozen ships in the mid-1960s, the Marseilles-based firm had a long and colourful history, dating from 1851. But, with rising costs under the French flag and increasing competition from less expensive foreign-flag competitors, Messageries Maritimes merged with Paris-based Compagnie Générale Transatlantique (CGT – the French Line) and together became Compagnie Générale Maritime. It was privatised and restyled as CMA-CGM in 1996, and has emerged as the world's third largest container ship operator in 2017.

China Navigation Co. Ltd

Based in Hong Kong, and part of the John Swire Group (which included links to Alfred Holt & Co. and therefore the mighty Blue Funnel Line), British-owned China Navigation ran their ships around as well as out of the Far East.

Post-World War Two rebuilding included no less than eighteen ships, eight of which were passenger-cargo ships: *Changsha*, *Taiyuan*, *Anking*, *Anshun* and, smallest of all, the 3,000-ton *Sinkiang*, *Szechuan*, *Shansi* and *Soochow*. The *Anking* and *Anshun* were originally designed specifically for a China coast–Singapore service, carrying Chinese labourers as well as perishable food items for cargo (in five holds). But because Chinese ports were closed in 1949, the forthcoming *Anking* and *Anshun* had to be promptly reassigned. While they served on various routes in the Far East (including rotating monthly sailings between Melbourne, Sydney, Brisbane, Port Moresby, Manila and Hong Kong), they were also used at times to take Chinese labourers out to the phosphate islands of the South Pacific and also to return overseas Chinese to Hong Kong so they could visit their ancestral homes on the mainland.

Gordon Cooper served as a junior officer aboard the *Anshun*. Built locally, by the Taikoo Dockyard & Engineering Co. in 1951, this 6,160grt ship was at the time the largest vessel built in Hong Kong since the Second World War (her sister ship the *Anking* was, however, constructed at far-away Greenock in Scotland). Gordon served for one year with China Navigation and was posted out to the Far East, to the 418ft-long, 14½-knot *Anshun*. 'Shipowners are in the business of earning money and making profits,' he recalled:

> So, the *Anshun* was chartered to the Malaysian Government for part of the year. The purpose: to carry pilgrims from Borneo and Malaysia to Jeddah for the Hadj. I made three of these voyages. We crossed to Mecca, offloaded the pilgrims and then, with crew only aboard, we crossed the Red Sea to Massawa in Ethiopia. It was an old Italian colonial port. We remained there for two or three weeks, until the Hadj was completed. And the reason: only so the crew could drink.

Crews on ships such as the Hong Kong-registered, single-screw *Anshun* were quite diverse. 'We had a South African captain', remembered Gordon Cooper, 'and British officers. The actual crew were Chinese and Malay. The pursers were Chinese and they looked after a thousand or more pilgrims during these voyages.'

Officially, the *Anshun* was listed to carry fifty first class in cabins, 116 in steerage in permanent berths and over 1,000 in steerage, in so-called 'portable berths':

The ship was chartered to the Malaysian Government so that lower-class Malaysians, village and hill people, could go to Mecca. While we carried doctors, there was also a 'witch doctor' on-board. The funnel of the ship was even repainted with the Malaysian flag. On one of my trips, we had 1,149 pilgrims on-board an otherwise smallish ship such as the *Anshun*. We carried them in the tween decks, in bunks that were three high. The bunks were really flat boards. The pilgrims brought along their own bedding or cushions or used clothing.

It was approximately $700 round-trip for each pilgrim. But this was paid for by the Government. During the voyages, some elderly would die. But pregnant women would give birth on-board and, according to custom and tradition, make *Anshun* the middle name. We would add 100 Malays as kitchen and cleaning staff. We set up several big kitchens and served only buffet style. There was also a tremendous need for fresh water and we added lots of faucets. Not only did the pilgrims have to bathe, but wash prior to prayers. These pilgrim-passengers were well behaved, but most of them smoked. They also hung clothing and other items to create privacy and these created massive fire risks. Only the children spoke some English and so, using candy, they were made fire wardens throughout the ship.

The forward and aft holds were used for the pilgrims' clothing, which was held in sacks and nets. For them, it was the trip of a lifetime. Unfortunately, once in Jeddah, they were ripped off by the Arabians. It was a long walk to Mecca and so they needed water for drinking and bathing. But the Arabs sold the water at high, often very high prices. They also needed goats and sheep for sacrifices. These were sold at very high prices as well.

During the voyages, there was no entertainment. The pilgrims spent most of the time sitting around, praying and attending prayer lessons. The passenger cabins were occupied by some middle-class Malays. But they were really quite basic, much like crew cabins. There was nothing fancy about them. The pilgrims joined the *Anshun* in ports such as Port Swettenham, Kuching, Penang and lots of smaller ports. Many of the pilgrims came from little villages and the ship would be leaning to one side as they waved to crowds on shore. Once, I remember the sultan came down to see the *Anshun* sail off. But the road had to be cleared and cleaned, and the pier strengthened to support the sultan's huge, all-white Rolls-Royce.

The pilgrim trade by ship dried up by the mid-1970s, being replaced by cheap air fares to Mecca.

Both the *Anshun* and *Anking* remained with China Navigation for some twenty years. Then, beginning in 1971, the *Anshun* did another twenty years with Pakistan's Pan-Islamic Shipping Co. as the restyled *Safina-E-Abid*. Again, she was in in the pilgrim trade. Indeed, she had a long life. Gordon Cooper's former ship was 40 years old when she was delivered to the breakers at Gadani Beach in Pakistan in April 1991.

Orient Overseas Line

Having very humble beginnings after World War Two, Hong Kong shipowner C.Y. Tung began buying second-hand freighters in the 1950s and 1960s. Under the Orient Overseas banner, services spanned the globe, including a round-the-world route: San Diego, Acapulco, Cristóbal, Port Everglades, La Guairá, Rio de Janeiro, Santos, Buenos Aires, Cape Town, Durban, Lourenço Marques, Dar es Salaam, Mombasa, Singapore, Hong Kong, Kaohsiung, Keelung, Kobe, Nagoya, Yokohama, Vancouver, San Francisco, Los Angeles and return to San Diego.

Orient Overseas began carrying containers in the late 1960s and today is one of the world's largest container-ship operators. It was reported, in 2017, that the company might be acquired by France's CMA-CGM.

Watching freighters: at San Francisco, States Marine Lines' *Golden State* on the left; *Maiden Creek* of the Waterman Steamship Co. on the right. (Gillespie-Faber Collection)

Maersk Line

When shipowner A.P. Moller entered the freighter trades in 1928, his success was steady. His Maersk Line became well known for their light blue hulls and

Maersk Line's *Nicoline Maersk,* attended by a Moran tug, arrives off Lower Manhattan and heads for her Brooklyn berth. (Gillespie-Faber Collection)

stars on their funnels. I remember that Maersk cargo liners were well known in New York Harbor for their blue hulls and the ships' names being painted along the sides. Two or three Maersk freighters called each week and often had special on-board facilities for Asian-made silks, reefer space and deep tanks for a variety of liquid goods.

Headquartered in Copenhagen, Maersk expanded in almost all aspects of shipping – from deep-sea tugs to super tankers. Maersk endured, kept pace with the times and shipping trends and would later acquire major competitors. They bought the likes of Safmarine Lines and Sea-Land Services in 1999, P&O-Nedlloyd in 2005 and Hamburg Sud in 2017.

By 2017, Maersk had an almost 20 per cent share of the international container trade. They have skilfully grown and expanded and, by 2017, Maersk ranked as the largest container cargo operator in the world.

Transition: The Container Age

Beginning in the 1960s, with the gradual shift of containerised cargo handling in New York Harbor, the waterway between Bayonne and Staten Island known as the Kill van Kull became increasingly busy. As container ships grew in size, their owners soon shifted to the more open facilities at Port Newark and Port Elizabeth in New Jersey (and also to Howland Hook on Staten Island). The face of New York (and later ports around the world) changed. Almost in a flash, classic freighters were gone, as were finger piers, cargo-laden barges and covered warehouses and sheds. The business of shipping also shifted from older, often inner harbours to more distant stretches of flatland, vast open spaces better suited to marshalling containers, trucking and big, bird-like cranes.

Officially, when the converted tanker *Ideal X* left New York on 26 April 1956, carrying fifty-eight cargo-laden truck-trailers on its specially fitted deck, containerisation was born. It would revolutionise the cargo handling business on the seas forever. This first container ship was the brainchild of North Carolina businessman Malcolm McLean, who bought his first second-hand truck back in 1934 and then steadily built up to a fleet of over 1,800 trucks – the largest in the American South. As early as 1937, however, he noted that there was considerable wasted time in handling cargo on and off ships. Stevedores took far too long in handling sacks of coffee and bales of cotton. He thought it much more practical to lift whole trucks on and off ships. He also wanted to save taxes and avoid waterfront theft as well.

Historically, Seatrain Lines on its New York–Havana run had carried railway freight cars – 'box cars', as they were called in America – on its ships beginning in 1929. But McLean envisioned an entirely new system: separating the truck container from its bed and wheels, and loading it aboard ship and then stacking these containers.

The container age – Sea-Land at Port Elizabeth, New Jersey. (Port Authority of New York & New Jersey)

TRANSITION: THE CONTAINER AGE   119

By the mid-1950s, McLean moved out of the trucking business, bought the Pan-Atlantic Tanker Company and soon reformed his operation as Sea-Land Shipping (then renamed Sea-Land Service, but later sold out to Denmark's giant Maersk Line). At first, the shipping industry cautiously watched McLean's operation, but soon realised its great efficiency and enormous cost savings. Great success and great expansion followed. Modern-day mega container ships (2017) can carry over 20,000 containers per voyage. The effect on worldwide trade has been extraordinary.

Large container ships are handled by tall, bird-like cranes that can 'swing' sixty or more containers per hour. Concurrently, everything in the port changed drastically with this system: barges and lighterage were no longer needed, turnaround times for ships changed from days to hours, and big, highly manoeuvrable container ships needed fewer and fewer tugs. By the 1970s, the face of ports around the world was dramatically different.

The shipping business itself also changed enormously. Once great and mighty shipping firms such as United States Lines, Moore-McCormack, British India, Ellerman, Harrison, Royal Rotterdam Lloyd, Hansa, Swedish American and Johnson Line have vanished, lost to maritime history books. These days, the biggest shipping owning and operating companies are often the result of mergers and acquisitions. Alone, and since the 1980s, Denmark's Maersk Line has incorporated the likes of Sea-Land, P&O, Nedlloyd, Safmarine and Hamburg Sud. Gordon Cooper suggests, 'Consolidation creates investor efficiency, which creates more money to invest.'

By early 2017, Germany's Hapag-Lloyd took over Chile's CSAV and was itself to merge with United Arab Shipping. Another German, Hamburg Sud, was expected to join Denmark's Maersk (and that will include one Brazilian and one Chilean container line as well). Japan's NYK, Mitsui and K Line were merging their operations, to become Ocean Network Express. France's CMA-CGM took over Singapore's Neptune Orient Lines, as well as their American President Lines division and was said to be wanting Hong Kong-based Orient Overseas Line.

In China, COSCO and China Ocean Shipping had merged. Elsewhere, Taiwan's Evergreen and Zim of Israel were said to be looking for partners, and Maersk and Mediterranean Shipping have a working agreement that includes two smaller Asian lines.

THE LARGEST CONTAINER COMPANIES IN 2017

Maersk	632 ships★	15.9% market share
MSC	481 ships	13.7% market share
CMA-CGM	449 ships	10.3% market share
China Ocean	290 ships	7.8% market share
Evergreen	188 ships	4.8% market share

(★Many Maersk ships are on charter and not owned outright)

—m—

On a spring evening in 2017, I was one of the narrators on a harbour cruise at the Port of New York. Always special to me, the port is always at work, active and changing. There were tugs handling oil barges, shuttling ferries and a big, bulky Japanese car carrier was passing under the Verrazano Bridge and heading out to sea. The purpose of our cruise, under the banner of the educationally themed Working Harbor Group, was to visit the vast New Jersey container docks and terminals at Port Newark and Port Elizabeth.

Four big container ships were in port – and several of them were still being 'worked' by mighty, bird-like container cranes. Two of the ships seemed huge and were over 900ft long. They were stacked high with coloured 'boxes', the containers. These four container ships were, we estimated, the equivalent of twenty or so freighters of the 1950s and 1960s. What a contrast, what a change.

As our boat and its 150 mostly camera-toting guests reversed course in order to depart, one of the container ships departed as well. She was stacked high with containers. But then, inbound and assisted by two tugs, was another giant container ship, also Japanese. She would be berthed by dark and, so we were told, offloaded and then loaded well into the night.

It is a busy and certainly more efficient age in shipping – 'in handling the cargo'.

Bibliography

Clarkson, John, Harvey, Bill, and Roy Fenton, *Ships in Focus: Blue Funnel Line* (Preston: Ships in Focus Publications, 1998).

Dunn, Laurence, *Passenger Liners* (Southampton: Adlard Coles Ltd, 1961).

Greenway, Ambrose, *Cargo Liners: An Illustrated History* (Barnsley: Seaforth Publishing Co., 2009).

Kludas, Arnold, *Damals auf der Unterelbe* (Bad Segeberg: Uwe Detlefsen, 1995).

Miller, William H., *Along the Waterfront* (Stroud: Amberley, 2016).

Moody, Bert, *Ocean Ships* (London: Ian Allan Ltd, 1964).

New York Port Handbook (New York City: Port Authority of New York & New Jersey, 1958–64).

Official Steamship Guide (New York: Transportation Guides Inc., 1963).

Scull, Penrose, *Great Ships Around the World* (New York City: Ziff-Davis Publishing Co., 1960).

Ships & the Sea (Milwaukee, Wisconsin: Kalmbach Publishing Co., 1950–60).

Towline (New York City: Moran Towing & Transportation Co., 1953–75).

Williams, David L., & Richard de Kerbrech, *Cargo Ships: A Color Portfolio* (Hersham: Ian Allen Publishing Ltd, 2007).

The History Press

The destination for history

www.thehistorypress.co.uk